IMAGES OF WAR
EARLY JET FIGHTERS

Forty years of aviation progress! This 1952 image shows an original 1912 Curtiss biplane owned and flown by US aviator Billy Parker being overtaken by a swept-wing F-86 Sabre jet fighter.

IMAGES OF WAR
EARLY JET FIGHTERS: BRITISH AND AMERICAN 1944–1954

RARE PHOTOGRAPHS FROM WARTIME ARCHIVES

LEO MARRIOTT

Pen & Sword
AVIATION

An imprint of
Pen & Sword Books Ltd
Yorkshire – Philadelphia

First published in Great Britain in 2018 by
PEN & SWORD AVIATION
an imprint of
Pen & Sword Books Ltd
Yorkshire – Philadelphia

Copyright © Pen & Sword Books Ltd 2018

ISBN 978-1-52672-777-0

The right of Leo Marriott to be identified as Author
of this work has been asserted by him in accordance with the
Copyright, Designs and Patents Act 1988.

A CIP catalogue record for this book is available
from the British Library.

All rights reserved. No part of this book may be reproduced or transmitted
in any form or by any means, electronic or mechanical including photocopying,
recording or by any information storage and retrieval system,
without permission from the Publisher in writing.

Typeset by Mac Style
Printed and bound in the UK by CPI Group (UK) Ltd, Croydon, CR0 4YY

Pen & Sword Books Ltd incorporates the imprints of
Pen & Sword Books Limited incorporates the imprints of Atlas,
Archaeology, Aviation, Discovery, Family History, Fiction, History, Maritime, Military, Military
Classics, Politics, Select, Transport, True Crime, Air World, Frontline Publishing, Leo Cooper,
Remember When, Seaforth Publishing, The Praetorian Press, Wharncliffe Local History,
Wharncliffe Transport, Wharncliffe True Crime and White Owl.

For a complete list of Pen & Sword titles please contact:

PEN & SWORD BOOKS LTD
47 Church Street, Barnsley, South Yorkshire, S70 2AS, United Kingdom
E-mail: enquiries@pen-and-sword.co.uk
Website: www.pen-and-sword.co.uk

or

PEN & SWORD BOOKS
1950 Lawrence Rd, Havertown, PA 19083, USA
E-mail: Uspen-and-sword@casematepublishers.com
Website: www.penandswordbooks.com

Contents

Glossary vi

Introduction vii

Chapter 1: Jet Engine Development 1

Chapter 2: British and Commonwealth Jet Fighters 14

Chapter 3: US Air Force Jet Fighters 51

Chapter 4: US Navy Jet Fighters 86

Chapter 5: A Good Idea at the Time 117

Photo Credits 133

Bibliography 134

Glossary

2TAF	2nd Tactical Air Force (RAF)	NATO	North Atlantic Treaty Organisation
AFB	Air Force Base	RAAF	Royal Australian Air Force
AI	Airborne Interception (radar)	RAE	Royal Aircraft Establishment
ANG	Air National Guard	RAF	Royal Air Force
BuAer	Bureau of Aeronautics (US Navy)	RAN	Royal Australian Navy
CAC	Commonwealth Aircraft Corporation (Australia)	RATOG	rocket-assisted take-off gear
DLI	Deck Launched Interceptor	RAuxAF	Royal Auxiliary Air Force
FAW	Fighter (All Weather)	RCAF	Royal Canadian Air Force
FB	Fighter Bomber	RLM	Reichsluftfahrtministerium
FEAF	Far East Air Force	RN	Royal Navy
FFAR	Folding Fin Aerial Rocket	RNVR	Royal Navy Volunteer Reserve
FG	Fighter Group	shp	shaft horse power (measure of a turboprop's power output)
ft	foot/feet. Unit(s) of Imperial measurement of distance	SNCASE	Société Nationale des Constructions Aéronautiques du Sud-Est
ft/min	feet per minute (relating to rate of climb)	US	United States
GE	General Electric	USAAC	United States Army Air Corps
HMS	His/Her Majesty's Ship	USAAF	United States Army Air Force (1941–1947)
kph	kilometres per hour	USAF	United States Air Force (from 1947)
lb/lbs	pound(s). Unit of Imperial measurement of weight	USMC	United States Marine Corps
lb.s.t.	Pounds static thrust (measure of the power output of a jet engine)	USN	United States Navy
MAP	Ministry of Aircraft Production	VF	US Navy Fighter Squadron
MCAS	Marine Corps Air Station	VMF	US Marine Corps Fighter Squadron
MDAP	Mutual Defense Assistance Program	VMP	US Marine Corp Photo Reconnaissance Squadron
MoS	Ministry of Supply		
NACA	National Advisory Committee for Aeronautics (US)		
NAS	Naval Air Squadron		

Introduction

Jet combat aircraft first appeared in the closing stages of the Second World War and at that time the German Luftwaffe held a commanding lead with both jet fighters and bombers in service. The British Gloster Meteor was operational and the Americans were just getting the Lockheed P-80 Shooting Star into service. In the period covered by this book Britain held a substantial lead in jet engine technology but the Americans, with their greater industrial resources, were quicker to bring new fighter designs into service and to build prototypes to investigate the advances available from captured German technology. By the end of the Korean War in 1953, American fighter aircraft were perhaps two years ahead of most comparable British aircraft, a lead they never relinquished. By 1954, prototypes of American supersonic fighters such as the delta-winged Convair F-102 Delta Dart and the revolutionary Lockheed F-104 Starfighter had flown, although in Britain the English Electric P.1A, a forerunner of the Lightning fighter, had also taken to the air.

The aircraft described in this book were known by various names and designations and it is therefore helpful to explain the systems used by the various nations, air forces and navies. British aircraft were normally given names although they would have various company designations. For example, the Meteor was the Gloster G.41 and the Vampire was the de Havilland DH.100. However, these designations were not normally used outside the company concerned. In the period under review, British military aircraft were built to an official specification that was identified by a prefix letter indicating the type of aircraft, a sequential specification number and the year in which the specification was issued. Thus the initial Meteors were built to specification F.9/40 (i.e. the ninth Fighter specification issued in 1940). Relevant prefixes as far as this book is concerned include E (Experimental), F (Fighter), and N (Naval aircraft). In some cases, particularly prototypes that saw little further development, the aircraft was not officially named but was referred to by its specification (e.g. Gloster E.1/44).

In the case of named aircraft, subsequent variants were designated by Mark numbers (e.g. Mk.I, Mk.II, Mk.V) and as variants proliferated, prefix letters were introduced to indicate the aircraft's role (e.g. F.Mk.XVI, PR.Mk.XIX). By 1945, with Spitfire/Seafire variants reaching the forties and Mosquitoes in the thirties, the use of Roman numerals became very cumbersome and a transition to Arabic numerals was made official. Thus the Mosquito TT. Mk.XXXIV became the TT.34 (TT – Target Tug). This system has endured to the present day.

The Gloster Meteor was the first British jet fighter, and entered operational service in July 1944.

On the other hand, the United States Air Force and its forerunners had from the early 1920s adopted a logical system whereby each aircraft type was identified by a letter indicating its role and a unique sequential number. A suffix letter indicated sub variants. Initially the letter P (for Pursuit) was applied to fighters but this was changed to F in 1947. For example, the Lockheed Shooting Star was designated P-80 (the 80th fighter design) and subsequent variants were the P-80A, P-80B, P-80C and so on, although the P was changed to F after 1947. Prefix letters X and Y stood for experimental prototypes and pre-production aircraft respectively (e.g. XF-86). In the 1920s and 1930s, many aircraft were not named and were solely referred to by their designations but by the Second World War and subsequently, names were more commonly applied (e.g. P-51D Mustang, F-86A Sabre) although even today, many aircraft are better known by their designations rather than the official name.

The US Navy adopted a different system, which additionally gave an indication of the aircraft manufacturer in the format letter/number/letter. The first letter indicated the type of aircraft (F for Fighter), the last letter the manufacturer, and in between was the sequential design number for that manufacturer. So, for example, the F9F (Panther) was the ninth fighter design by Grumman (F being the letter allocated to Grumman). In the case of the first design by a manufacturer there was no number, such as with the North American FJ (Fury). In all cases, successive variants were indicated by a hyphenated number and sometimes with an additional

America's first operational jet fighter was the Lockheed P-80A Shooting Star. It was redesignated as the F-80A in 1947.

The US Navy's Vought XF7U-3 Cutlass illustrates the advances made in jet fighter design by the early 1950s.

suffix letter to indicate a specific role. A good example is the McDonnell F2H-2N Banshee, a specialised night fighter version of this aircraft.

Although outside the period covered by this book, it should be noted that the US Air Force and Navy systems were combined into a unified standard system in 1962, which resulted in the manufacturer's letter being dropped and some aircraft being redesignated. For instance, the Douglas F4D-4 Skyray became the F-6A.

In this book the power output of a jet engine is stated in terms of pounds static thrust. Jet engine efficiency increases with altitude whereas a piston engine's output gradually falls off as an aircraft climbs, although it can be boosted by supercharging. Consequently it is difficult to express an exact correlation between a jet engine's thrust rating and a piston engine's horse power. Very roughly, one pound of thrust is equivalent to one horse power but this only applies to a particular speed and altitude band of approximately 375mph at 15,000 feet. Faster and higher, then there is a progressive differential in favour of the jet engine.

Chapter One

Jet Engine Development

The father of the aeronautical jet engine is generally accepted as the British engineer and RAF officer Sir Frank Whittle, who patented the basic concept in January 1930. In fact, although Whittle's patent set out clearly for the first time the basic principles of a practical jet aero engine, there were many inventors and engineers who had previously demonstrated various theories and components that were ultimately incorporated in the first jet engines.

However, none of that should detract from Whittle's original thinking, which was greatly aided by the fact that he was himself a highly skilled pilot as well as an engineer. Unfortunately, his initial approach to the Air Ministry was rebuffed and he had to rely on a small band of

Sir Frank Whittle, the British pioneer of jet propulsion, is shown congratulating test pilot Gerry Sayer on completion of the maiden flight of the Gloster E.28/39, 15 May 1941. *Jet Age Museum, Gloucester.*

private investors to develop his ideas. With their support he formed Power Jets Ltd and a successful test bed run of his first working jet engine, known as the WU (Whittle Unit), occurred in April 1937. Even then it was not until 1939 that an order was placed for a flyable jet engine to power an experimental aircraft, the Gloster E.28/39, which eventually first flew on 15 May 1941. Although this was a highly significant event others had already taken on Whittle's ideas and had put them into practice. The German engineer Hans von Ohain had started work on his own ideas for a jet propulsion system and subsequently became aware of Whittle's patent. Supported by the aircraft manufacturer Ernst Heinkel, he had a demonstration engine running by September 1937, only a few months after Whittle's first engine had run. Ohain's first engine was fuelled by hydrogen but the subsequent HeS.3 used conventional fuels and produced a healthy 1,100lb.s.t. Around this engine Ernst Heinkel designed the He.178, which first flew on 27 August 1939 – the first jet-powered aircraft to fly and almost two years before the British E.28/39. Other German companies had also initiated work on jet engines in 1939 and these programmes resulted in the BMW 003 and Junkers Jumo 004 engines, both of which featured multi-stage axial compressors.

Heinkel also produced the He.280 twin-engined jet fighter, which flew on 2 April 1941, but the RLM preferred the rival Messerschmitt Me 262, which was to be powered by the

A sectioned Whittle W.2B jet engine showing the internal workings. Air is drawn in by the double-sided centrifugal compressor on the right and forced outwards into the ducts leading to the reverse-flow combustion chambers. Here the air is heated and exhausted at very high pressure through the blades of the turbine (at centre left), forcing it to rotate at high speed and so drive the compressor to which it is connected by a rotor shaft. *ASM photo*

A sectioned example of a German Jumo 004 axial-flow engine. Air is drawn in through the multiple compressor stages on the right, then through the combustion chambers before exhausting through the single-turbine rotor on the left. This arrangement resulted in an engine of much smaller cross-section, hence reduced drag, and one that was very efficient in operation. *ASM photo*

Jumo 004 engines. Development had started as early as 1938 but delays with producing suitable engines meant that its first jet-powered flight did not occur until 18 July 1942. Fortunately for the Allies, the Me 262 did not begin to reach operational units until the end of September 1944, by which time it was too late to significantly change the course of the air war. Nevertheless, the Me 262 was a remarkable aeroplane – fast, heavily armed and the first jet fighter to feature sweepback of the wings.

As well as the Me 262, by the end of the war in Europe in May 1945 Germany also had the four-engined Arado 234 jet bomber in service, and the single-engined He 162 jet fighter was in full production but was too late for operational service. Other advanced jet-powered aircraft existed in prototype or project form and these only came to light when Allied forces overran Germany in the spring of 1945. British, American and Russian technical teams rushed to salvage what they could both in terms of material and personnel. Captured aircraft were tested and evaluated and the Allies realised that they had lagged far behind in the application of jet technology. The results of German wartime experience and research were quickly applied to the design of new British and American jet aircraft. That such a situation had come about was almost entirely due to the lack of official support accorded to Whittle during his early attempts to build a practical jet engine. Even when things improved under the impetus of war, commercial infighting and duplication of effort still caused delays.

Britain's first jet aircraft, the Gloster E28/39, as completed in April 1941 but before a standard camouflage paint scheme and serial number W4041 had been applied. *Jet Age Museum, Gloucester*

With its swept-back wings, the Messerschmitt Me262 was best performing jet fighter of the Second World War. Captured examples were exhaustively tested by Allied pilots after the war.

The advent of jet-powered bombers such as the wartime German Arado 234 was a major factor in the development of post-war jet fighters.

As far as the British were concerned the experimental Gloster E.28/39 quickly proved the practical advantages of the jet engine. Although the initial Whittle W.1 engine was rated at only 860lb s.t., the aircraft was faster at altitude than a contemporary Spitfire. In fact, even before the E.28/39 had flown, the Air Ministry issued specification F.9/40 for a jet fighter and this led to the development of the twin-engined Meteor, which made its first flight on 5 March 1943. This event had been delayed for several months due to the lack of suitable engines, which in turn was the result of the chaotic approach to jet engines.

The Meteor was to be powered by an improved W.2 engine, which Whittle and Power Jets would design but would be produced by other established engineering companies, notably Rover. Unfortunately, relationships between Whittle and Rover deteriorated, each blaming the other for the various problems that arose, and progress was slow until in November 1942 the Rolls-Royce engineer Stanley Hooker arranged for that company to take over the development and production of Whittle engines. At that time the first examples of the redesigned W.2B/23 had been produced and by mid-1943 it was in production as the 1,600lb.s.t. Rolls-Royce Welland I. A Meteor powered by these engines first flew on 12 June 1943, but was not the first Meteor to fly.

In 1941, Sir Geoffrey de Havilland and his aero engine specialist Major Frank Halford witnessed the early flights of the Gloster E.28/39. Impressed by what they saw, they obtained

DG202/G was the first F.9/40 Meteor to be completed but, due to delays with the production of Whittle engines, was not the first to fly. *Jet Age Museum, Gloucester*

The Avro Lancastrian was a transport version of the Lancaster bomber and several were modified to act as testbeds for the new jet engines. This one was modified in 1947 by replacing the outer Merlin engines with streamlined nacelles to accommodate de Havilland Ghost turbojets. *P. Gilchrist collection*

Air Ministry approval to develop and produce their own jet engine, and with the resources of a major company available, progress was rapid. The Halford H.1 engine was running as early as April 1942 and subsequently demonstrated up to 3,000lb.s.t. on test. Continuing delays to the Whittle/Rover W.2B engines led to the fifth prototype, F.9/40 Meteor (DG206), being modified to accept two airworthy H.1 engines and it was this aircraft that had made the first Meteor flight on 5 March 1943. The H.1 engine, subsequently named Goblin, differed from the Whittle engines in several important respects. The centrifugal compressor was single-sided and the combustion chambers were of the straight-through-flow type as opposed to the Whittle design with a double-sided compressor and reverse-flow combustion chambers. This made for a simpler and more efficient engine and the production Goblin I was initially rated at 2,300lb.s.t. by September 1943, whilst the improved Goblin II was producing 3,000lb.s.t. by July 1945. By that time the enlarged H.2 Ghost was being tested at 4,000lb.s.t., increased to 4,850lb.s.t in later versions.

In the meantime, Rolls-Royce had redesigned the Welland to incorporate straight-through combustion chambers and with other modifications this became the Derwent I, rated at 2,000lb.s.t., which powered the Meteor F.3, the first major production variant. As has ever been the case with jet engine development, there has always been a demand for more and

The Rolls-Royce Nene first ran in October 1944 and, rated at 5,000lb.s.t., was the most powerful jet engine in the world at that time. Although based on Whittle's principles, it differed by having straight-through combustion chambers, as shown in this cutaway example. It was manufactured under licence in America by Pratt & Whitney as the J42 and Soviet-made copies powered the ubiquitous Mig-15. *ASM photo*

more thrust, and in early 1944 the MAP issued a specification calling for a jet engine producing a minimum of 4,000lb.s.t. Rolls-Royce responded with a new engine, the RB41 Nene, which by the end of the year was already running at no less than 5,000lb.s.t — making it the most powerful jet engine in the world at that time.

Following the first bench tests of the Nene, Whittle and some Rolls-Royce engineers, including Hooker, met in a local pub and in the ensuing conversation it was suggested that a scaled-down Nene could be produced for the Meteor. Less than six months later, by June 1945, this was produced as the Derwent 5. The new engines increased the Meteor's top speed by over 100mph and uprated versions were used in the Meteors that set new world speed records in 1945/46.

By 1945, Rolls-Royce and de Havilland were producing powerful and very reliable jet engines in quantity but Power Jets had been nationalised in April 1944, Whittle himself being reduced to the role of consultant, although still owning many important patents. However, other companies were involved in jet engine development, including Metropolitan-Vickers, which had a background in producing steam turbines. A test rig axial-flow engine was run as early as October 1940, whilst the definitive F.2 with a nine-stage compressor was first run in December 1941. Following flight tests in a Lancaster test bed, two 1,800lb.s.t. F.2 engines powered the third prototype Meteor (DG204), which first flew on 29 June 1943. Due to the slimmer profile of the axial-flow engines they were mounted in underwing nacelles. Subsequently the engine was renamed Beryl (after the precious stone, not the girl!), and with a ten-stage compressor, power output was gradually raised to 4,000lb.s.t. by 1945. In 1946, Dr D.M. Smith (Metrovick's head of engine development) designed the F9 Sapphire with a thirteen-stage compressor. This first ran in 1948, initially at around 7,000lb.s.t. but subsequently to over 11,000lb.s.t., although by that time, Metrovick had been forced out of the aero engine business and the Sapphire project was handed over to an established aero engine producer, Armstrong Siddeley.

With Germany defeated in 1945, Britain became for a time the world leader in jet propulsion, and even today, Rolls-Royce is one of three major producers of jet engines. The Tizard scientific mission to the United States in September 1940 explained British scientific advancements in various technologies including radar, atomic energy and jet propulsion. In regard to the latter, very little detailed information was passed on but it was enough to cause General 'Hap' Arnold, Chief of Staff of the USAAC, to press NACA to investigate the possibilities of jet propulsion. Arnold himself visited the UK in March and April 1941, and was given access to Whittle's work and viewed the E.28/39 prototype. Moving fast he arranged for the Whittle W.1X — Power Jet's only test engine — to be flown out to America together with a set of detailed drawings for the more advanced W.2B. On arrival in early October, these were passed on to the General Electric Company, who were well placed to develop jet engines having much experience of steam turbines for power generation and had also worked on turbo superchargers for aero engines. GE immediately set to work on building their own version of the W.2B, which was known as the Type I (I for India) and began test runs in April 1942. In June, Whittle visited America and suggested some improvements to the GE engine, which then became the Type I-A, rated at 1,250lb.s.t. In the meantime and even before the Whittle engine had arrived in America, Arnold contracted the Bell company to design and build a jet fighter based on the new jet engines. The result was the Bell XP-59, which first flew on 2 October 1942 – America's first jet fighter and, it should be noted, flown five months before the first Meteor. Although the XP-59 was a poor performer and was only produced in small numbers, the rapid pace of its development was a clear indication of the capabilities of the American aviation industry.

General Electric continued to develop the basic Whittle design and successively produced a series of engines in which thrust was gradually increased to 2,000lb.s.t. in the I-20 respectively. However, the USAAF was looking for more powerful engines in the 4,000lb.s.t. bracket and in response GE developed the I-40, which began testing in January 1944, subsequently demonstrating 4,200lb.s.t. America's first operational jet fighter was to be the Lockheed Shooting Star and the prototype XP-80 had flown on 8 January 1944, powered by a British Halford H.1B jet engine rated at 2,460lb.s.t. However, by that time it had been decided that all subsequent P-80s would be powered by the I-40 (now designated J33) and this required some redesign of the airframe to accommodate the larger engine.

General Electric also began work on an axial-flow turbojet, the TG-180, although

General Henry 'Hap' Arnold, Chief of the US Army Air Corps, visited Britain in the spring of 1941 and was able to see Whittle's work at first hand. He was instrumental in encouraging American companies to develop and produce jet engines.

The Bell XP-59 Airacomet was America's first jet fighter and actually flew before the British Meteor.

The Lockheed P-80 was designed so that the whole tail section could be easily removed in order to access the engine, as shown here, where the arrangement of the straight-through combustion chambers of the Allison J33 engine is visible.

The more powerful J35 turbojet was developed by General Electric but responsibility for production was transferred to Allison in September 1946. Its first application was in the Republic XF-84 Thunderjet.

the design of the combustion chambers was based on Whittle's work. This first ran in April 1944, producing 3,620lb.s.t., later increased to 4,000lb.s.t. when, as the J35, it powered the prototype Republic XF-84 on its maiden flight (28 February 1946).

However, by that time General Electric was being divested of many of its jet developments and production of the J33 was handed over to Allison in September 1945, followed by the J35 twelve months later, these moves being initiated to set up Allison as a competitive provider of jet engines and to utilise that company's spare production capacity. Nevertheless, General Electric continued to work in the field and developed a new engine based on the J35 but with an additional compressor stage. This became the J47, which first ran in June 1947, and from an initial rating of 4,850lb.s.t. it was constantly improved until the last production variant (J-47-33) gave 7,650lb.s.t. with afterburning.

One American company that relied less on British input was the Westinghouse Electric Corporation. As interest in the possibilities of jet propulsion began to stir in 1941, Westinghouse was encouraged by the US Navy to work on their own design for an axial-flow engine, with a formal contract being signed on 8 December, the day after Pearl Harbour. It was a relatively small engine with a maximum diameter of 19 inches and consequently was designated 19A. Westinghouse envisaged its use as a booster for conventional aircraft but also planned that it could be scaled up or down to 24 or 9.5 inches, the latter possibly powering guided missiles. The first X19A, and first American designed jet engine, ran on test in March 1943, demonstrating a thrust rating of 1,200lb.s.t. Originally it had a six-stage axial compressor but the X19B had ten stages, and as the J30 it powered the US Navy's first jet fighter, the McDonnell XFD-1 Phantom. The 24-inch diameter engine was also developed as the J34, with an eleven-stage compressor and produced 3,000lb.s.t. (later increased to 3,400lb). It was produced in quantity from 1947 for the US Navy's F2H Banshee and Douglas F3D Skyknight jet fighters.

The General Electric J47 was a highly successful engine and powered many US military aircraft of the period, including the F-86 Sabre and the B-47 Stratojet bomber. No less than 36,500 J47 turbojets were produced up to 1956. *ASM Photo*

Westinghouse had a prototype X19A axial-flow engine delivering 1,200lb.s.t. running by March 1943. In January 1944, one was attached under the Goodyear FG-1 Corsair shown here for testing.

Eager to build on its relationship with the US Navy, Westinghouse went ahead with new designs including the J40, which first ran in October 1948 and was the power plant of choice for several navy projects including the A3D Skywarrior attack bomber, the F4D delta-wing interceptor, the F3H Demon fighter and XF10F swing-wing fighter. However, the engine was a total failure and proved very unreliable. This had a very detrimental effect on all of these major aircraft projects and although the first three were eventually modified with different engines, the revolutionary XF10F was cancelled. This disaster effectively put Westinghouse out of the jet engine business as none of its subsequent designs achieved any success.

When the US Navy decided on the Rolls-Royce Nene engine to power its new Grumman F9F Panther it tasked Pratt & Whitney with setting up an American production line and also adapting it for easier production using American systems and engineering methods. By 1948, the engine now designated J42, was in full production and rated at 5,750lb.s.t. (with water injection). Further collaboration with Rolls-Royce resulted in an improved version, which Rolls named the Tay and was the J48 in US service. Although the parent company did not market the Tay, it was used by the US Navy to power later versions of the Panther (F9F-5) and its swept-wing derivative the Cougar (F9F-6), and also by the USAF in the F-94 Starfire all-weather fighter.

In 1950, the Curtiss Wright Corporation also turned to Britain and purchased a licence agreement to produce the Armstrong Siddeley Sapphire as the Wright J65. Delays caused by adapting and modifying the engine meant that deliveries did not commence until 1953. It subsequently powered the very successful Douglas A4D Skyhawk as well as the Grumman F11F Tiger, Martin B-57 Canberra and the Republic F-84F Thunderstreak.

By the mid-1950s, the end of the period covered by this book, Britain was still a world leader in jet engine development but the American companies were flexing their muscles, and

The prototype Grumman XF9F-2 Panther first flew in November 1947 and most early production Panthers were powered by the Pratt & Whitney J42, a licence-built version of the Rolls-Royce Nene.

with greater financial and industrial resources were soon to pull ahead. The situation was not helped by the fact that in the coming decades the US Air Force and Navy were to order substantial quantities of new high-performance supersonic combat aircraft such as the navy's F8U Crusader and F4H Phantom II, and the air force's Century series fighters such as the F101 Voodoo and the F104 Starfighter. These aircraft all demanded substantial advances in jet engine technology, a stimulus that was lacking in Britain, which ultimately produced only one home-grown supersonic combat aircraft, the English Electric Lightning. Today, Rolls-Royce is still a front-rank aero engine company but its production is geared towards the civil market, and any military engines are produced in partnership with international consortiums.

American supersonic fighters under development during the 1950s, like this McDonnell F-101 Voodoo, provided the incentive for a new range of jet engines such as the General Electric J79 and Pratt & Whitney J57, offering well in excess of 10,000lb.s.t. *ASM photo*

Chapter Two

British Jet Fighters

The original specification for Britain's first jet, the Gloster E.28/39, required provision that the aircraft could form the basis for an 'interceptor fighter'. However, Gloster's chief designer George Carter quickly realised that the early jet engines were not powerful enough and proposed that any new fighter would have to be twin-engined. The Air Ministry agreed and Specification F.9/40 was written around his proposals. Notable features included wing-mounted engines, a forward positioned cockpit (later with a full clear-view bubble canopy) and a tricycle undercarriage, while a fin-mounted tailplane was adopted to keep it clear of the hot jet efflux. Armament comprised four 20mm cannon. Problems with production of suitable engines delayed the first flight until 5 March 1943, by which time the name Meteor had been adopted. A total of twelve F.9/40s prototypes had been ordered, although only eight were actually completed, and even before these had flown an initial batch of twenty Meteor F.1s was ordered in August 1941. The first of these flew in January 1944, powered by two Rolls-Royce W.2B/23 Welland rated at 1,700lb.s.t., which resulted in a maximum speed of 430mph and a service ceiling of 42,000 feet. These figures were not that much in excess of contemporary piston-engined fighters except at higher altitudes, where the jets were considerably more efficient.

The Meteor F.1 entered service with 616 Squadron in July 1944 and was subsequently based at Manston, where it scored some successes against the German V-1 missiles then targeting London. In January 1945, the squadron moved to Nijmegen in Belgium but hoped-for encounters with the German jets did not occur, and by April 1945 the Meteors were operating over Germany in the ground-attack role. Before deploying overseas, 616 Squadron had re-equipped with the Meteor F.3, which featured a number of improvements including a strengthened airframe, speed brakes and increased fuel capacity. The first fifteen F.3s retained the Welland engines but the 195 production F.3s that followed were powered by the 2,000lb.s.t. Rolls-Royce Derwent, which offered some improvement in performance. By the end of 1945, the Meteor F.3 was entering widespread service with Fighter Command and eventually served with twelve front-line squadrons as well as RAuxAF squadrons. However, development continued and the first Meteor powered by the new Rolls-Royce Derwent V took to the air on 17 July 1945. Initially rated at 3,500lb.s.t., this engine almost doubled the installed power with a consequent dramatic increase in performance. The resulting production Meteor F.4 was capable of 585mph (Mach 0.77) at sea level and 540mph

The first Meteor to fly was the fifth F.9/40 prototype but was powered by Halford H.1 engines due to delays with the intended Whittle units. *Jet Age Museum, Gloucester*

The first operational Meteor squadron was 616, which became operational in July 1944, initially with early F.1s but upgrading to F.3s before moving to Belgium in January 1945. A second squadron, 504, was operational by March 1945. Next to receive the new jets, but not until August 1945, was 124 Squadron, and three of their F.3s are shown here still wearing wartime camouflage and code letters. *ASM collection*

With more powerful Derwent 5 engines, the Meteor F.4 offered a substantial increase in overall performance when it entered service in May 1945. The example shown here belonged to 74 Squadron, which began re-equipping with this variant in December 1947.

(Mach 0.81) at 30,000 feet. Service ceiling was a staggering 52,000 feet and this sort of performance was way ahead of anything else flying at the time.

Entering service in 1946, the Meteor F.4 quickly replaced earlier variants and went on to serve with twenty-three front-line and auxiliary squadrons. It was also widely exported, but despite this success the Meteor was already becoming outperformed by other aircraft and so in 1947, development of the Meteor F.8 was initiated. This would be the final day fighter version of this ubiquitous aircraft and the first prototype flew on 12 October 1948. It was Australian Meteor F.8s that were the first to see action since the Second World War and the first to engage in jet air-to-air combat. No.77 Squadron RAAF, serving in Korea, re-equipped with the Meteor F.8 in February 1951 but subsequently it proved no match for the enemy swept-wing Mig-15 and was relegated to ground-attack duties, a task that it performed well.

The Meteor proved to be a very adaptable airframe and was produced in several versions, including a two-seat trainer (T.7), photo reconnaissance (FR.9 and PR.10) and night fighter (NF.11 to NF.14). As already mentioned, it was a great export success, a vital boost to the British economy in the post-war years and was built under licence in Belgium and the Netherlands.

The Meteor was not the only potential jet fighter produced by Gloster. Problems with delivery of early jet engines led to the possibility of an alternative single-engined design being developed under specification E.1/44. The prototype was not completed until July 1947 and then was almost destroyed in a road accident while being delivered to Boscombe Down for flight trials. The second prototype did not fly until 9 March 1948. Powered by a 5,000lb.s.t. Rolls-Royce Nene, it was very fast, achieving 620mph, and also demonstrated a good rate of climb. Despite the aircraft's potential, further development was cancelled in 1949 shortly after the third example had flown.

Following the Meteor into service was the single-engined de Havilland Vampire. Development began in 1942 and a twin-boom layout gave rise to the name Spider Crab, which was later changed to Vampire after the prototype flew on 20 September 1943 powered by de

In November 1945, a modified Meteor F.3 had set a World Air Speed Record of 606mph and on 7 September 1946, an F.4 raised this to 616mph. The latter, EE549, flown by Group Captain Donaldson, is shown passing the timing point at the start of the 3km course off the Sussex coast. *ASM collection*

Havilland's own Goblin engine (originally known as the Halford H.1), rated at 2.700lb.s.t. Production of an initial batch of Vampire F.1s was sub-contracted to English Electric at Preston and Salmesbury in Lancashire, and their first aircraft flew on 20 April 1945. Deliveries to the RAF did not begin until April 1946 but by the end of that year three squadrons (Nos. 247, 54 and 130) forming the Odiham Wing had all re-equipped with the new jet fighter. The F.1. had a maximum speed of 540mph and a range of 730 miles on internal fuel. The Vampire was easy to fly and was popular with its pilots although it required a long take-off run and rate of climb was substantially less than that of the Meteor F.4.

The Meteor F.8 featured a stretched fuselage, reduced wingspan and a new angular fin and tailplane. Range and endurance were improved by an increase in fuel tankage but overall performance was only marginally superior to the F.4. Nevertheless, the F.8 rapidly replaced the F.4 in the RAF and was widely exported. The example shown here is one of twenty delivered to the Royal Danish Air Force in 1951.

The third E.1/44 prototype, which featured a raised tailplane, similar to that of the Meteor F.8, the other two having a fuselage-mounted tailplane. *Jet Age Museum, Gloucester*

This early production Vampire F.1 clearly shows the twin boom arrangement, which allowed a short jet pipe and raised the tailplane above the hot exhaust.

Immediately after the war, the Society of British Aircraft Constructors (SBAC) organised their annual air show at Radlett, the Handley Page airfield north of London. De Havilland here proudly display a Vampire F.1. at the 1946 event. *P. Gilchrist collection*

The Vampire F.2 was powered by a Rolls-Royce Nene engine, which required additional air intakes for its double-sided compressor. This version was never produced for the RAF but served as a basis for Vampires subsequently produced in France and Australia. Shown here is the prototype Australian Vampire F.Mk.30, which first flew in June 1948.

The Vampire F.3, first flown on 4 November 1946, had the more powerful Goblin 2 engine and could carry long-range drop tanks. This enabled a formation of six 54 Squadron Vampire F.3s in July 1948 to become the first jets to cross the Atlantic, staging through Iceland, Greenland and Goose Bay in Canada. Subsequently they visited various Canadian and American airfields and are shown here at Greenville AFB on 26 July.

Based at RAF Odiham, 247 Squadron began replacing its Vampire F.3s with the FB.5s, shown here in late 1949, and operated in the ground-attack role. *Aviation Photo Library*

The next production version was the Vampire F.3, which flew in prototype form on 4 November 1946 and was powered by the Goblin 2 engine, developing 3,100lb.s.t. This version was ordered in large numbers and quickly replaced the earlier F.1 in front-line service. In turn, the F.3 was soon replaced by the Vampire FB.5, which was effectively an F.3 with strengthened wings to allow for the carriage of two 1,000lb bombs or eight rocket projectiles. A later version was the FB.9, modified for service in the Middle and Far East by the provision of air conditioning for the cockpit. Production of single-seat Vampires ended in December 1953, by which time a total of 1,565 Vampires had been delivered to the Royal Air Force and Royal Navy, although some of these had been passed on to other air forces. In fact, the Vampire was a major export success and customers included Sweden, Canada, South Africa and Venezuela, whilst licence production of Goblin-powered Vampires was undertaken in Switzerland and Italy. In Australia, CAC produced a total of eighty modified Vampires (F.30 and FB.31) powered by the 5,000lb.s.t. Rolls-Royce Nene engine, which raised top speed to 570mph. France also set up production lines and SNCASE delivered 183 standard FB.51s and 250 Nene-powered aircraft known as the Mistral.

The availability of the more powerful de Havilland Ghost jet engine, rated at 4,850lb.s.t., led to a redesign of the Vampire to take advantage of the increased power. The most obvious difference was a new thin section wing with a swept-back leading edge, which was stressed to allow the fitting of 75gal wing tip tanks. The revised aircraft was renamed as the DH.112 Venom and the prototype flew on 2 September 1949. Despite some initial handling problems and the need to strengthen the wing structure, the Venom subsequently became a well liked and successful ground-attack fighter. Initial production version was the FB.1, which entered

The de Havilland DH.112 Venom was a straightforward development of the Vampire with a thinner wing featuring a swept back leading edge. It was also the first RAF fighter to carry wing tip fuel tanks. This is the second prototype, which flew on 23 July 1950. *ASM Collection*

A Venom FB.1 starting up, the plume of smoke coming from a starter cartridge, which was commonly used in the early jet era. This aircraft belongs to a 2nd TAF squadron based in Germany, and in addition to the nose-mounted 20mm cannons, the underwing rocket launcher rails are visible. *PRM Aviation Collection*

service in 1952 with 2TAF squadrons in Germany and from 1954 equipped RAF squadrons in Cyprus and the Middle and Far East. The improved FB.4 prototype flew on 29 December 1953, and as well as being fitted with hydraulic aileron controls for improved handling at high Mach numbers, it also featured an ejector seat. This last item was much appreciated by RAF pilots and was retrofitted to many FB.1s. With a top speed of 640mph and a rate of climb of 9,000ft/min, the Venom offered a considerable advance on the Vampire, which it quickly replaced in front-line service from 1955 onwards and some remained in service as late as 1962. Several were built for export, the main customer being Switzerland, which ordered 140 FB.1s and 100 FB.4s, and the last of these were only retired in 1983.

On 3 December 1945, a modified Vampire became the first jet ever to land on an aircraft carrier. However, despite the success of these trials the Vampire was deemed not suitable for regular service with the Fleet Air Arm. The main problem was the slow response of the early jet engines in the event of a wave off resulting in a dangerous delay before enough thrust was

There was early naval interest in the de Havilland Vampire, and on 3 December 1945, Lieutenant Commander Eric Brown made the first landing by a jet aboard an aircraft carrier, HMS *Ocean*. The aircraft involved was LZ551/G, the second prototype Vampire, modified for deck landings. *National Museum of the Royal Navy*

The Royal Navy ordered twenty Sea Vampire F.20s, which were strengthened for deck landings and fitted with an arrester hook. However, they did not have folding wings and were mostly land based for jet familiarisation training, although some were occasionally deployed at sea for exercises. This example was flown by 771 NAS, a Fleet Requirements Unit based at Ford in Sussex from 1952. *Aviation Photo Library*

In 1948, the Royal Navy together with the RAE investigated the possibility of operating aircraft without undercarriages (to save weight) using a rubber landing deck and transferring the aircraft to a catapult trolley for take-off. A number of suitably modified Sea Vampire F.21s carried out a series of trials at Farnborough prior to successful demonstrations aboard the carrier HMS *Warrior* in 1949. Although the idea worked, the concept was not pursued. *National Museum of the Royal Navy*

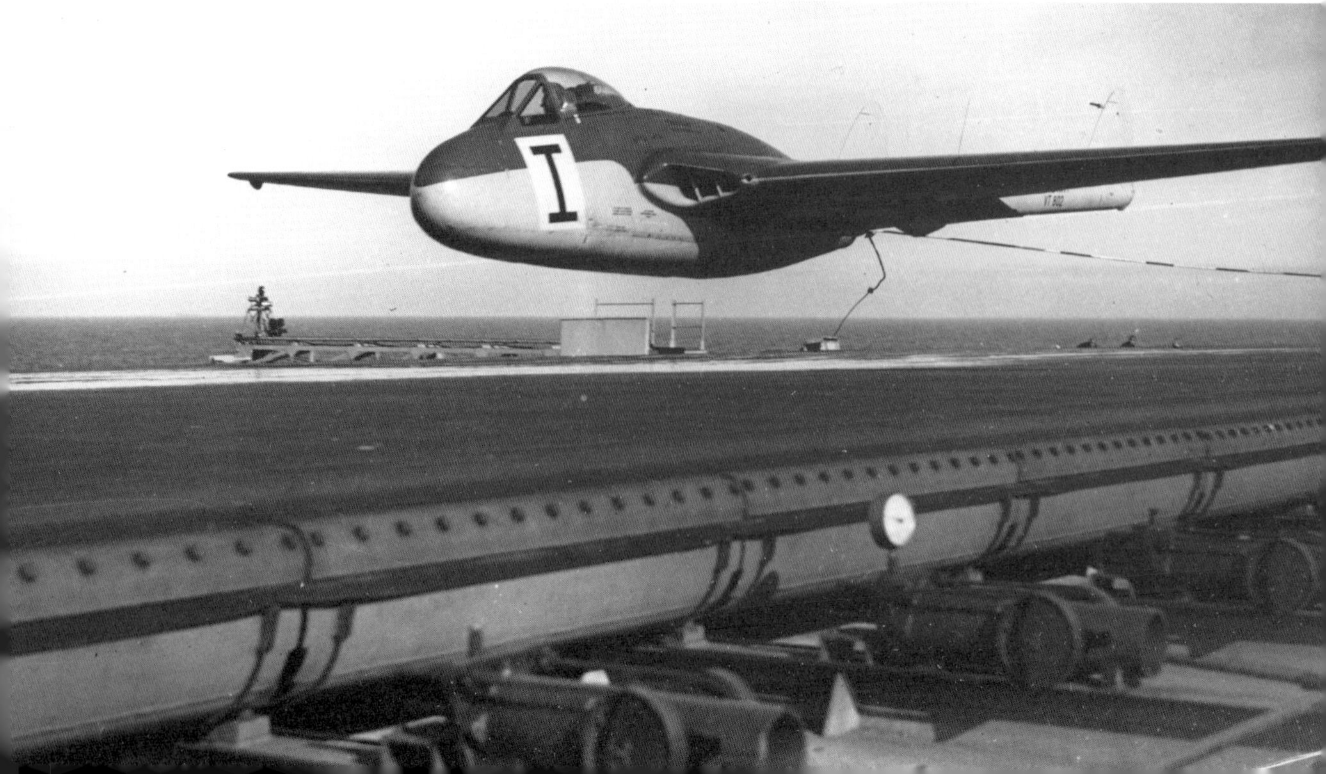

available to safely climb away. Nevertheless, a small number of navalised Vampire F.20s were ordered and the first were delivered in 1947.

In 1944, Supermarine had flown a developed version of the famous Spitfire known as the Spiteful, which featured a new laminar flow wing and a wide-track inwardly retracting undercarriage. One Spiteful recorded a speed of 494mph in level flight, which was the highest ever attained by a British piston-engined aircraft. A naval version known as the Seafang successfully completed carrier suitability trials in 1945, but by then the Royal Navy was actively considering the acquisition of a jet fighter. Supermarine suggested using the Spiteful's laminar flow wing as a basis for a jet fighter around which the MAP raised specification E.10/44, later amended to E.1/45 for a naval version. Initially referred to as the 'Jet Spiteful', the name Attacker was adopted when the first E.10/44 prototype flew on 27 July 1946. The first fully navalised Attacker, with folding wings and an arrestor hook, was flown in June 1947 but it was not until the following year that an initial order for sixty aircraft was forthcoming, with deliveries commencing in 1950. The Royal Navy's first operational jet fighter squadron was formed in August 1951 and later embarked on the newly commissioned HMS *Eagle* in March 1952. The Attacker was always regarded as an interim aircraft and its front-line service with the Royal Navy was relatively brief, with the last squadron disbanding in 1955 although

The prototype Supermarine F.10/44 (TS409) airborne from Boscombe Down during the early flight test programme. The navalised version became the Attacker, the Royal Navy's first fully operational jet fighter. *ASM Collection*

A good view of an early production Attacker F.1. Although the prototype had flown as early as 1946, deliveries of production aircraft did not commence until 1950. Note the extended dorsal fin, a modification incorporated from early 1951.

One reason for the slow delivery of jets to the Royal Navy was the lack of a suitable carrier from which they could operate. This was rectified in late 1951 when the 43,000 ton HMS *Eagle* commissioned. *ASM collection*

Full house! Supermarine Attackers of 800 NAS, the Royal Navy's first operational jet fighter squadron, ranged forward aboard HMS *Eagle* in early 1953.

An Attacker FB.2 being prepared for a catapult launch from American carrier USS *Antietam* during angled deck trials carried out in the English Channel in 1953.

Pilot's eye view. Like most early jets the Attacker's cockpit was not dissimilar from that of the piston-engined fighters it replaced. At top centre is the gyro gunsight also used for aiming rocket projectiles and below which are the six instruments of the standard British blind flying panel.

it did continue with RNVR units until 1957. A total of 149 were built for the Royal Navy and the only export order was from the Pakistan Air Force, which took delivery of thirty-six.

Although specification E.10/44 was framed around Supermarine's proposals, rival company Hawker submitted its own design as a private venture. This aroused naval interest and under specification N.7/46 three prototypes were ordered. The resulting Hawker P.1040 first flew on 2 September 1947, and the first fully navalised example almost exactly a year later (3 September 1948). Like the Attacker, the P.1040 (now named Seahawk) was powered by a 5,000lb.s.t. Rolls-Royce Nene turbojet and although it offered a similar performance, it was regarded as a more sophisticated and flexible aircraft. The folded wingspan was considerably less than the Attacker and a tricycle undercarriage made deck handling much easier. The Seahawk entered service with 806 NAS in March 1953 and subsequently served with thirteen front-line squadrons as well as several RNVR and training squadrons. Initially produced as an interceptor fighter, it was subsequently developed as a fighter bomber and a total of 434 were delivered to the Royal Navy, all but the first thirty-five being produced by Armstrong Whitworth, a subsidiary of the Hawker Siddeley Group. The Seahawk also achieved significant export success, being produced for Germany (sixty-four ordered), the Netherlands (twenty-two) and India (seventy-four), although some of the latter were refurbished ex-RN aircraft.

The prototype Hawker P.1040 (VP401) served as an aerodynamic prototype for the Seahawk but was not equipped for naval operations. Note the squared-off fairing for the jet exhaust.

The second Seahawk prototype (VP413) was fully navalised with catapult spools, folding wings, arrester hook and an armament of four 20mm cannon. This aircraft and production Seahawks featured the tapered 'pen nib' jet exhaust fairings.

Will it fit? During 1949, Seahawk VP413 carried out a series of trials aboard HMS *Illustrious*, as a result of which it was found necessary to increase the wingspan by 30 inches to improve low speed handling. *ASM collection*

Close-up of a Seahawk preparing for a catapult launch. Positioned well forward, the pilot has an excellent field of view – an important attribute for a carrier-based aircraft. Note the gun ports for the 20mm cannon.

One of 35 Hawker-built Seahawk F.1s. All subsequent Seahawk development and production was transferred to Armstrong Whitworth at their Coventry factory.

Even before the Seahawk entered service the Admiralty were considering a faster and heavier twin-engined fighter. This had its origins in a scheme to operate aircraft without undercarriages (saving space, weight and allowing thinner wings) using the flexible deck concept for landing. Supermarine proposed the Type 505, a twin-engined jet with straight wings and a Vee tail. The flexible deck concept was abandoned by 1947 and so the design was altered to include a conventional tricycle undercarriage. The result was the Type 508 and the navy ordered three prototypes to Specification N.9/47 (later also known as N113), the first of these flying from Boscombe Down on 31 August 1951. At that time it was the largest and heaviest aircraft produced for the Royal Navy but powered by two 6,500lb.s.t. Rolls-Royce Avon axial-flow engines, it had a good turn of speed and an exceptional rate of climb. However, by that time Supermarine had already experienced the benefits of swept wings and the third prototype (VX138) was redesigned to incorporate this feature to become the Type 525. Other changes included a conventional swept fin and tailplane, and more powerful 7,500lb.s.t. Ra.7 Avon engines were installed, making this the most powerful fighter in the world when it took to the air on 27 April 1954. Nevertheless, it remained stubbornly subsonic due to the high drag rise approaching Mach 1. This was a problem also experienced in America, where in 1952 aerodynamicist Richard Whitcomb evolved the concept of area rule in which an aircraft is designed such that its overall cross-section area, including the wings, gradually increases to a maximum and then falls away smoothly along the length of the aircraft. Subsequent development of the Type 525 into the Type 544 Scimitar included a redesigned fuselage incorporating area rule, but even with two 10,000lb.s.t. Avon Ra.24s it was only capable of Mach 0.98 in level flight, although supersonic in a shallow dive.

The Supermarine Type 508 prototype (VX113) shows off its clean lines and Vee tail during a low pass at Chilbolton during early flight trials towards the end of 1951.

The Type 508 carried out successful carrier trials aboard HMS *Eagle* in 1952/53. With its two Rolls-Royce Avon jet engines it was probably the most powerful naval fighter of its day and demonstrated excellent performance. *National Museum of the Royal Navy*

The third prototype (VX138) ordered under the N.9/47 specification differed substantially from its predecessors and was given the company designation Type 525. The most obvious difference was the introduction of swept wings and a conventional cruciform tail assembly with swept surfaces. This aircraft was subsequently destroyed in a crash on 5 July 1955.

Development of the Type 525 eventually resulted in the Type 544 Scimitar, which flew in 1956 but did not enter service with the Royal Navy until 1958, eleven years after the original N.9/47 specification.
ASM collection

Immediately after the war, Supermarine and Hawker had both produced single-engined jet fighters that had not been accepted by the RAF but had proved suitable for naval service. Both companies continued to develop and refine the Attacker and Seahawk, notably by the application of swept wings and more powerful engines with the result that both eventually saw service with the RAF as the Swift and Hunter respectively. Specification E.41/46 was issued for the construction of two Supermarine Type 510, which was essentially an Attacker with new swept wings and tail surfaces. First flown on 28 December 1948, speeds of over 600mph were quickly demonstrated although handling problems at both ends of the speed range were apparent. However, it was thought to offer the basis for a useful jet fighter and the second prototype, which had flown in March 1950, was returned to the factory for major modifications, notably an extended nose to accommodate a tricycle undercarriage. In this guise and redesignated as the Type 535, it took to the air on 23 August 1950. All these development aircraft were powered by a standard Rolls-Royce Nene engine although the Type 535 also had an afterburner system, the first and only such application to the Nene. By this time the name Swift had been adopted and the outbreak of the Korean War in June 1950 gave impetus to its development as an operational fighter. This was the Type 541, in which the Nene was replaced by the 7,500lb.s.t. Rolls-Royce Avon Ra.7 and which flew in prototype form on 1 August 1951. Despite the increased power the Swift was not capable of supersonic flight due to control problems at speeds in excess of Mach 0.91, but these were eventually

VV106 was the first of two Supermarine Type 510, in which the basic Attacker airframe was mated to a new swept wing.

Although a sleek and streamlined aircraft, the Type 510 still retained the Attacker's tail wheel undercarriage. *ASM collection*

In November 1950, VV106 was modified by the addition of an arrester hook and an uprated undercarriage in order to carry out carrier trials aboard HMS *Illustrious*. In so doing it became the first swept-wing jet to land on an aircraft carrier. *National Museum of the Royal Navy*

The second Type 510 prototype (VV119) differed slightly and incorporated afterburning for the Nene jet engine. Consequently it was redesignated as the Type 528 and flew briefly in this form in March 1950. However, it was further modified by lengthening the nose to allow a tricycle undercarriage to be fitted, the wing root trailing edges had reduced sweepback to increase wing area, and the tail cone was lengthened and tapered. In this form it became the Type 535, shown here, and formed the basis for the subsequent Swift fighter.

solved in late production aircraft by the introduction of powered flying controls and an all-flying tailplane, and even the second prototype became the first example to exceed the speed of sound in a dive on 26 February 1953. The Swift became the first British swept-wing jet to enter service, equipping 56 Squadron in February 1954. However, operational experience revealed that a loss of control was experienced when manoeuvring at speeds above Mach 0.85 and efforts to solve this problem met only partial success. As a result the Swift was withdrawn from front-line service although it did subsequently perform well in the low-level fighter reconnaissance (FR) role, equipping two squadrons from 1956 until 1960.

On the other hand, Hawker were to have much more success with their developments based on the naval P.1040 Seahawk. As early as 1945, Hawker submitted a proposal for a swept-wing version and two prototypes were ordered as the P.1052 in May 1947 to specification E.38/46. The first prototype (VX272) flew on 19 November 1948, but during its career suffered several forced landings and spent much time under repair. The second prototype (VX279) flew on 13 April 1949, and was involved in various research programmes until April 1950, when it was returned to Hawkers for conversion to the Hawker P.1081. This was as the result of an enquiry from the RAAF in respect of a possible fighter version of the

The Swift F.1 and F.2 (shown here) were produced in small numbers and equipped 56 Squadron from February 1954, but were later withdrawn. In May 1953, a Swift F.4 gained the World Air Speed Record with a speed of 735.7mph over a measured course off the Libyan coast at Tripoli. *ASM collection*

Two prototypes of a swept-wing P.1052 were ordered in May 1947, and the first of these flew on 19 November 1948. The basic layout of the Seahawk was retained, including the tail assembly with its unswept tailplane. However, the swept wings imparted a substantial increase in maximum speed and serious consideration was given to ordering it into production. *ASM collection*

VX272, the first P.1052 prototype, had a chequered career involving at least two forced landings. The resulting repairs and modifications delayed carrier trails aboard HMS *Eagle* until May 1952, and although these were successful, no production order was forthcoming. *ASM collection*

In April 1950, the second P.1052 (VX279) underwent a substantial reconstruction and emerged as the P.1081, making its first flight in this form on 19 June 1950. Based on a possible Australian order for a swept-wing jet fighter, the P.1081 had a straight through jet pipe instead of the original bifurcated exhausts and new swept tail surfaces. VX279 is shown here during a press briefing at Heathrow but was later lost in a fatal accident on 3 April 1951.

P.1052 and for which Hawker proposed the use of a Rolls-Royce Tay engine to replace the Nene. However, the Australian project was cancelled in November 1950 and the aircraft was handed over to the RAE for further trials.

In 1947, Hawker began work on a new interceptor powered by the new Rolls-Royce Avon turbojet under the designation P.1067. This attracted official interest and specification F.3/48 was drawn up, leading to a contract for three prototypes in June 1948. The name Hunter was adopted and even before the first prototype had flown on 20 July 1951, orders for 200 Avon-powered Hunter F.1s had been placed with Hawker Aircraft Ltd and 200 Sapphire-powered Hunter F.2s from Armstrong Whitworth at Coventry. These substantial orders resulted from the urgent need to re-equip the RAF's fighter squadrons as a result of the outbreak of the Korean War in 1950. An innovative feature of the Hunter was its heavy armament of four 30mm cannon contained in a detachable gun pack under the forward fuselage.

The Hunter F.1 entered service with the RAF in July 1954, but almost immediately problems were encountered when the guns were fired at high altitude as this caused compressor surging and even flameouts in the Avon engines, although the Sapphire engined F.2 did not experience this problem. The Avon engine problems were mostly solved with the Hunter F.4, which entered service in 1955, and this version as standard had underwing hard points for drop tanks or bombs (the Sapphire-engined equivalent was the F.5). The ultimate interceptor Hunter was the F.6 powered by a 10,000lb.s.t. Avon RA28, which entered service in late 1956 and gradually replaced the earlier marks in RAF front-line squadrons. Overall, the Hunter was enormously successful and much loved by its pilots. It was also produced in trainer and

Although bearing a superficial resemblance to the P.1081, the Hawker P.1067 Hunter was an entirely separate project designed around specification F.3/48. The prototype (WB188) first flew on 20 July 1951, by which time orders for 400 aircraft had already been placed. Subsequently this aircraft was fitted with a more powerful Rolls-Royce Avon engine as the sole Hunter F.3 and established a World Air Speed Record of 727.6mph on 3 September 1953.

An early production Avon-powered F.1. The F.2 was similar except that it was powered by an Armstrong Siddeley Sapphire turbojet.

specialised ground-attack variants, and a total of 1,028 were delivered to the RAF. Export orders flooded in and the Hunter was built under licence by Fokker in Holland and Avions Fairey in Belgium, who between them built 460 Hunter F.4s and F.6s for their respective air forces. Substantial deliveries from British factories were made to Sweden, Denmark, Switzerland and India, as well as various Middle East and South American air forces.

In the immediate post-war era there was an urgent need to produce a jet-powered night fighter and the initial response was to produce versions of the Meteor and Vampire/Venom. The RAF's first choice was the Meteor, for which specification F.24/48 was issued to cover production of a two-seat night fighter version. The Meteor NF.11 first flew on 31 May 1951 and featured a longer nose to accommodate the A.I radar and space for a radar operator/navigator seated in tandem behind the pilot. Displaced by the radar, the four 20mm cannon were moved to the wings outboard of the engines and a Meteor F.8 tail assembly was fitted. To maintain altitude performance of the heavier night fighter, long-span wings were fitted. NF.11s entered service in August 1951, initially with 29 Squadron but subsequently with six Fighter Command squadrons and six RAF Germany squadrons.

The Meteor NF.12 was similar but had an improved radar, and the NF.13 was a version optimised for tropical service. The final variant was the NF.14 (first flown October 1953), which was recognisable by its clear-view unframed canopy and was actually 17 inches longer than the NF.11. A total of 556 night fighter Meteors were delivered, all produced by Armstrong Whitworth at Coventry, who were also responsible for the design changes

A Gloster Meteor NF.11 belonging to 151 Squadron, which re-equipped with the night fighter Meteor in April 1953 having previously flown the Vampire NF.10. *ASM collection*

Final production version of the Meteor was the NF.14, which was distinguished externally by its clear canopy and slightly longer nose. The example shown here is in the markings of 85 Squadron, based at West Malling in Kent, which flew NF.14s from 1954 until 1958.

required. Meteor night fighters were gradually replaced from 1956 onwards, but the last front-line squadron (No.60 FEAF) retained its NF.14s until 1961.

Although the Meteor was the RAF's prime choice for operation as a night fighter, it was not the first to enter service. De Havilland had developed a two-seat, radar-equipped version of the Vampire under the designation DH.113, which first flew on 28 August 1948. Intended for the export market, twelve were ordered in 1949 by the Egyptian Air Force but subsequently the export of arms to Egypt was banned and these aircraft, together with later production, were taken over by the RAF. The first of these entered service with 23 Squadron in July 1951, just a month before the first Meteor NF.11s became operational. Ultimately, three squadrons flew the Vampire NF.10 but by early 1954 they had all been replaced either by Meteors or the de Havilland Venom NF.2/3. A few Vampire night fighters were delivered to the Italian Air Force as the NF.54 whilst many refurbished RAF aircraft were supplied to the Indian Air Force in 1957–58.

The Venom NF.2 was a logical development of the Venom that had already replaced the Vampire as a day fighter. Again a company private venture, the prototype two-seat Venom NF.2 flew on 22 August 1950 and offered substantial performance improvements over the Vampire. Maximum speed rose from 538mph to 595mph and initial rate of climb from 4,500ft/min to 6,450ft/min. Entering service with 23 Squadron in November 1953, it subsequently equipped up to eight Fighter Command Squadrons from then until November 1957.

The de Havilland DH.113 Vampire NF.10 entered service with the RAF in July 1951 as an interim measure pending delivery of twin-engined Meteor night fighters. This example is in the markings of 23 Squadron. *Aviation Photo Library*

The de Havilland DH.112 Venom night fighter was also a private venture but was adopted by the RAF after trials at Boscombe Down during 1951. Photo shows WP227, the prototype Venom NF.2. Later production versions (NF.2A and NF.3) had an improved clear-view canopy.

A pair of Venom NF.2s displaying the distinctive red and blue markings of 23 Squadron based at RAF Coltishall. This unit had previously flown the Vampire NF.10 but converted to the more advanced Venom night fighter at the end of 1953. *PRM Aviation Collection*

The Royal Navy also had a requirement for a radar-equipped night fighter and after evaluation of the Venom NF.2 prototype, it ordered an initial batch of twenty Sea Venom FAW.20s. Some were issued to 890 NAS in March 1954 but these were replaced by the improved FAW.21 before embarking for carrier operations. The FAW.21 had power-operated ailerons, a new clear-view canopy, a long-stroke undercarriage and, significantly, introduced ejector seats for the crew. The final production version was the FAW.22, which had the more powerful 5,300lb.s.t. de Havilland Ghost 105 engine. Sea Venoms served with eight RN front-line squadrons until December 1960, as well as with three trials and training units. The RAN ordered thirty-nine Sea Venom FAW.53s, which flew from the carrier HMAS *Melbourne* from 1956.

For both the RAF and RN, the Meteor, Vampire and Venom night fighters were always regarded as interim aircraft pending the delivery of purpose designed two-seat, all-weather fighters, whose development began as early as 1946. By the early 1950s, traditional pursuit course interceptions had been replaced by collision course tactics in which the fighter flew directly towards the bomber from a head-on or beam position. In this case the time available for opening fire and destroying the bomber would be very limited, possibly only a matter of seconds with high closing speeds. Conventional gunfire would be ineffective unless heavy calibre guns were used and solutions considered included large guns up to 127mm calibre, salvoes of unguided rockets (FFAR), and guided missiles. All of these required a sophisticated radar system coupled to an automated fire control system, which would be used irrespective of day/night and weather conditions. Aircraft that could be operated in this manner were

After a Royal Navy evaluation of the prototype Venom NF.2, the second prototype (WK376, shown here) was completed in a semi-navalised form, strengthened for catapult launching and fitted with an arrester hook. In this form it carried out successful carrier trials aboard HMS *Illustrious* in July 1951. *Aviation Photo Library*

Entering front-line service in March 1954, the production Sea Venom FAW.20 featured power-operated folding wings. Later variants were the FAW.21 and FAW.22, which had a clear-view canopy, improved radars, ejector seats and uprated Ghost engines. Here an 809 NAS FAW.21 launches from HMS *Albion* in 1957. *Andy Ford Collection*

known as all-weather (AW) fighters as opposed to the earlier night fighter (NF) terminology, which implied a less sophisticated capability.

In 1948, the RAF issued specification F4/48, which called for a radar-equipped interceptor capable of over 600mph with a service ceiling of 45,000 feet and a rate of climb such that this altitude could be reached within ten minutes of commencing engine start on the ground, and both Gloster and de Havilland had already investigated designs that might meet this specification. When the results of German experimentation with delta wings became available, Gloster proposed that this configuration be adopted. On the other hand, de Havilland developed its tried and tested twin-boom layout but upgraded with swept wings and twin engines. Both designs utilised axial-flow engines but whilst de Havilland chose the Rolls-Royce Avon, Gloster adopted the Armstrong Siddeley Sapphire. First to fly, on 26 September 1951,

The Gloster Javelin two-seat, all-weather fighter was evolved to meet specification E.4/48 and its distinctive feature was the broad delta wing. A total of five prototypes were ordered, the first of which (WD804) flew on 26 November 1951. *Jet Age Museum, Gloucester*

Showing the delta-wing planform is the third prototype (WT827), which flew on 7 March 1953 and was the first to carry armament (four wing-mounted 30mm cannon) and an AI radar, which was contained in an experimental blunt nose cone. This was later changed to the pointed nose cone as fitted to production aircraft. *Jet Age Museum, Gloucester*

was the de Havilland DH.110, closely followed on 26 November by the prototype delta-winged Gloster Javelin. After comparative trials in 1952, the RAF chose the Javelin but development was hampered by indecision on the part of the MoS. Eventually the first four prototypes had flown by January 1954. The first was seriously damaged in a high-speed landing following a loss of elevator control and the second completely destroyed and the pilot killed when it failed to recover from a superstall – a condition not previously encountered by any jet aircraft. Due to these setbacks and the need to incorporate various modifications including a revised wing planform, production aircraft did not reach an operational squadron (No.46) until February 1956. Subsequent development of the Javelin is outside the scope of this book but it is worth noting that early versions were armed only with four 30mm cannon, but in 1958, the Javelin FAW.7 armed with Firestreak air-to-air missiles entered service. A total of 427 Javelins were produced for the RAF, which equipped fourteen squadrons, and it remained in service until 1967.

The de Havilland DH.110, which had lost out to the Javelin in the 1952 evaluation, was still of interest to the Royal Navy and in July 1952, de Havilland modified their design to meet an updated N14/49 specification. Again, the subsequent history of the aircraft, which became the Sea Vixen, really lies outside the period covered by this book, but to conclude the story,

The first of forty production Javelin FAW.1s flew on 22 July 1954, but many were allocated for trials and development flying and consequently, the first operational unit (46 Squadron) did not form until February 1956. The example shown here (XA546) had a very short career, crashing into the Bristol Channel on 21 October 1954 after the pilot was unable to recover from a spin.

The de Havilland DH.110 was originally designed to meet the same Air Ministry specification as the Gloster Javelin. The first prototype (WG236) flew on 26 September 1951, and in the following April exceeded the speed of sound in a shallow dive. Unfortunately, this aircraft was lost in an horrendous accident at the 1952 Farnborough Air Show when it broke up during the display routine, killing the pilot and observer as well as many spectators on the ground. *P. Gilchrist collection*

The second DH.110 (WG240) flew on 25 July 1952, but following the loss of the first aircraft it was grounded for modifications and did not fly again until June 1954. The Royal Navy was now interested in developing it as a carrier-based, all-weather fighter and in September 1954, WG240 was used for a series of demonstration touch-and-go landings aboard the light fleet carrier HMS *Albion*. Although painted in naval colours, this aircraft was not fitted with an arrester hook or folding wings.

Subsequently development of the DH.110 resulted in the de Havilland Sea Vixen FAW.1, which eventually entered front-line service with 892 NAS in 1959. The lengthy timescale was due to the fact that production of the Sea Vixen required an 80 per cent redesign of the original DH.110. *ASM collection*

a semi-navalised third prototype was completed in June 1955 and this carried out carrier trials aboard HMS *Ark Royal* in April 1956. It was not until 1957 that 700 NAS received the first production aircraft for trials, and the first operational squadron (892 NAS) did not form until the summer of 1959. A total of 114 Sea Vixens were produced and the type remained in service until 1972.

During the Second World War, Canadian companies produced aircraft such as the Mosquito and Lancaster. One was the National Steel Car Corporation, whose Aircraft Division subsequently became Victory Aircraft Ltd, which by 1945 had delivered over 400 Lancasters. In December 1945, Avro, designers of the Lancaster, took over the factory and set up a new company, A.V.Roe Canada Ltd, whilst in 1946 they acquired Turbo Research Ltd, which had been working on jet engine development since 1944. The new company was thus able to respond to an RCAF requirement for a two-seat, twin-engined, jet-powered, all-weather fighter. This became the CF-100 Canuck, which first flew on 19 January 1950, over a year before the RAF's similar Meteor NF.11. The first two CF-100 prototypes were powered by a pair of Rolls-Royce Avon engines but ten unarmed pre-production Mk.2s were powered by indigenously developed Avro Canada Orenda engines rated at 6,000lb.s.t. Deliveries of the Mk.3, armed with eight 0.5in machine guns housed in a quick-change ventral pack, began in September 1952. In October 1953, the first Mk.4A flew, and in this variant the ventral gun pack could be replaced by a battery of unguided 2.75in rockets and a further twenty-nine rockets could be carried in each of the wing tip pods. A new APG-40 radar and MG-2 fire-control system was installed to facilitate collision course tactics using the unguided rocket batteries. The later Mk.4B had uprated 7,300lb.s.t. Orenda 11 engines, and although the CF-100 was not

The second of two CF-100 Mk.I prototypes. Both were finished in this all-black colour scheme with white flashes and lettering. Subsequent production aircraft had a natural metal finish.

as fast as some contemporary fighters, it had an excellent rate of climb (7–9,000 ft/min depending on the variant) and offered a genuine all-weather capability. Final version was the Mk.5, which featured an increased wingspan for improved high altitude performance, although this did not reach operational squadrons until 1956. Avro Canada achieved export success when Belgium chose the CF-100, fifty-three Mk.5s being delivered.

As a tailpiece on this chapter about British fighter development in the period 1944–54 it is worth recording that the prototype English Electric P.1A made its first flight on 4 August 1954. This was the forerunner of the P.1B Lightning fighter, which eventually became operational in June 1960 – the first and only all-British fully supersonic combat aircraft.

First flown on 4 August 1954, the English Electric P.1A subsequently formed the basis for the P.1B Lightning, which eventually entered service in 1960.

Chapter Three

United States Air Force Jet Fighters

The first American jet fighter was the Bell XP-59 Airacomet. The contract for the construction of three prototypes was placed in September 1941, immediately following General Electric's contracts to produce jet engines based on the Whittle designs. Bell's design was fairly conventional with a straight-wing, tricycle undercarriage, and two GE Type I-A jet engines mounted in nacelles under the wing roots. Although design and construction of the prototype proceeded rapidly, completion was delayed by the late delivery of suitable engines. Despite this, the XP-59 made its first flight from Muroc dry lake (later Edwards AFB) on 1 October 1942, five months before the prototype Meteor. Subsequently the USAAF ordered

Following an initial request from the USAAF in September 1941, the Bell Aircraft Corporation designed, built, and flew the prototype XP-59A Airacomet in just over twelve months.

Production P-59A Airacomets were armed with a single 37mm cannon and three 0.5in machine guns. The example shown here (422610) was actually the second production P-59A and was allocated to the 412th Fighter Group in 1944 for training and jet familiarisation purposes.

Some thirty P-59Bs were produced, which differed only in having additional fuel tanks in the outer wing panels. One of these is shown in May 1945 at Santa Maria Army Airfield in California, where it is carrying out an engine run, the hot jet exhaust dramatically visible in the evening light.

thirteen pre-production YP-59s, which featured a sliding cockpit canopy to replace the original sideways hinging unit and were intended to be powered by the more powerful 1,600lb.s.t. GE Type I-16 jet engine. However, the first few YP-59As had to make do with the Type I-A, with which maximum speed at 35,000 feet was 389mph, although this increased to 409mph when fitted with the I-16 engines. This was not a startling performance and eventually only 50 P-59A and P-59B Airacomets were delivered by August 1945, when production ended, and many of these equipped the 412th Fighter Group, which had been established in November 1943. This unit was formed to familiarise pilots and ground crew with jet operations and was never intended to engage in combat operations.

By 1944, experience in the European air war showed the need for long-range fighters to escort bomber formations. Accordingly, Bell looked at a derivative of the P-59 to undertake this role. Compared to piston-engined fighters, jets used considerably more fuel, and so although the Bell long-range fighter designated XP-83 was loosely based on the preceding P-59, it was much larger and featured a deep fuselage to allow installation of additional fuel tanks. It was powered by two General Electric J33 centrifugal-flow jet engines rated at 4,000lb.s.t., which resulted in a maximum speed of 522mph and a service ceiling of 45,000 feet. The first of two prototypes flew on 25 January 1945, but overall performance was disappointing and no production orders were forthcoming.

The first really practical jet fighter to reach air force squadrons was the Lockheed P-80 Shooting Star. As early as 1940, Lockheed had started development of a jet engine known as the L-1000, and around this they designed a canard-winged fighter, but the engine proved too complex for the time and the project was abandoned. However, because of this experience

The Bell XP-83 was designed as a long-range escort fighter. Although similar in concept to the earlier P-59A, it featured a bulky fuselage to accommodate fuel tanks containing 912 gallons (Imperial), which could be supplemented by underwing tanks to give a maximum range of 2,050 miles.

A ground view of 484990, the first of two XP-83 prototypes which flew on 25 February 1945. Projected armament would have been six 0.5in machine guns or four 20mm cannon.

The Lockheed P-80 Shooting Star was America's first fully operational jet fighter although was just too late to see service in the Second World War. This is a P-80A (485004), from the initial production batch, many of which were finished in the overall light grey paint scheme. Subsequent P-80s reverted to a natural metal finish.

Lockheed were asked in May 1943 to design a fighter using the British 3,000lb.s.t. Halford H.1B. turbojet. The subsequent contract, issued on 24 June, specified that the first prototype, now designated XP-80 Shooting Star, should be completed within 180 days. The company beat this by a substantial margin but flight testing was delayed by the late delivery of a flight-cleared Halford engine. With this installed the XP-80 took to the air on 8 January 1944 and subsequently demonstrated a top speed of 502mph. However, in September 1943 it was decided that production aircraft would be powered by the 4,000lb thrust General Electric I-40 (later produced as the J33) and modifications to accommodate the larger engine resulted in a contract for two XP-80As. The first of these flew on 10 June 1944 and was more representative of production aircraft with increased fuel capacity and an armament of six 0.5 inch machine guns. These were followed by thirteen YP-80As, of which two were deployed to Italy in the spring of 1945 for demonstration and familiarisation purposes, although they were not used in action.

During 1944, almost 5,000 P-80s were on order or planned, but with the end of the war in September 1945, these numbers were substantially reduced. Nevertheless, a total of 1,731 P-80 Shooting Stars were delivered from 1944 to 1949, these comprising three main variants (all of which were redesignated F-80 from 1947 onwards). The P-80A was the initial production version, powered by a General Electric J33-GE-11 rated at 3,850lb.s.t. or a 4,000lb.s.t. Allison J33-A-17. Entering service in 1947, the P-80B featured a thinner wing, an ejector seat and faster firing M-3 machine guns. In 1946/47, the prototype XP-80B was

In July 1948, a squadron of the 56th Fighter Group made a successful West-East Atlantic crossing staging through Newfoundland, Greenland and Iceland. Their P-80A Shooting Stars are shown after arrival at RAF Odiham. Unfortunately, the prestige of the first jet Atlantic crossing had already been claimed a few days earlier by RAF Vampires of 54 Squadron.

Powered by an uprated Allison J33-A-23, the Lockheed F-80C was the final production version, and many earlier aircraft were upgraded to the same standard for issue to ANG units. Shown here is a formation of F-80Cs flown by the 36th FB Squadron, 8th FB Wing. Note the prominent 'Buzz Numbers', of which the first letter indicates the role (F for Fighter), the second allocated to a specific type (in this case T for the F-80), and the last three numbers of the aircraft's serial number.

modified and prepared for an attempt on the World Air Speed Record, then still held at 615.8mph by the Gloster Meteor. After several attempts it finally succeeded on 19 June 1947 with a speed of 623.738mph, which was also significant as it was the first time the record had been set at over 1,000kph. Final production version was the heavier P-80C fitted with more powerful Allison J33 engines, offering thrust ratings of between 4,600 and 5,400lbs. A number of A and C variants were modified for the photographic reconnaissance role by removing the guns and fitting cameras in a modified nose. Initially known as FP-80s, these subsequently became RF-80s under the new designation system. The F-80 was heavily involved in the Korean War but almost exclusively in the ground-attack or reconnaissance roles, although the first victory in a jet versus jet combat was claimed by Lieutenant Russell J. Brown, who shot down a Mig-15 on 7 November 1950 while flying an F-80C Shooting Star (although Russian records do not support this). The last operational USAF F-80s were withdrawn in 1958, but many ex-USAF aircraft were transferred to South American air forces, who continued to fly them well into the 1970s. A two-seat trainer version of the Shooting Star was the T-33, of which 5,691 examples were produced from 1948 onwards for the USAF, US Navy and numerous overseas air forces.

The relatively uncluttered cockpit of an F-80C Shooting Star.

The FP-80A (later redesignated RF-80A) was a photo reconnaissance version of the Shooting Star with cameras mounted in an extended nose. These examples are flown by the 363rd Reconnaissance Wing, based at Langley AFB, in 1948.

Republic started work on a jet fighter in 1944, which eventually became the XP-84 Thunderjet, and the orange painted prototype took to the air on 28 February 1946.

The P-84B (later F-84B) was the first production version and entered service with the 14th FG, based at Dow Field, Maine, in the summer of 1947.

When Republic began looking at the idea of a jet-powered fighter they initially considered fitting an axial-flow turbojet in a modified P-47 Thunderbolt, but this idea was soon abandoned and a new design was prepared. The resulting XP-84 Thunderjet was an exceptionally clean design with a very slim fuselage, taking full advantage of the smaller diameter of the J35 axial-flow engine. Due to this configuration, most of the fuel capacity was built into the relatively thick unswept wing. The prototype flew on 28 February 1946 and quickly demonstrated a maximum speed of just over 600mph, slightly faster than the Lockheed P-80. It was powered by a General Electric/Allison 3,750lb.s.t. J35-GE-7 turbojet but the subsequent YF-84As had the J35-A-15, rated at 4,000lbs thrust. The production F-84B entered service with the 14th Fighter Group in mid-1947, and subsequent variants were the F-84C, F-84D and F-84E. These featured incremental improvements, with engine thrust improving to 5,000lbs in the F-84E and maximum loaded weight rose from 15,800lbs to 22,000lbs (or 24,000lbs with RATOG – rocket-assisted take-off gear). These figures allowed the F-84 to act as an effective ground-attack aircraft carrying a variety of ordnance, including rocket projectiles and 1,000lb bombs. The ultimate production Thunderjet, introduced in 1951, was the F-84G, which was equipped to carry tactical nuclear weapons (the first single-seat fighter bomber to have this capability). Powered by a 5,600lb.s.t. J33-A-29 engine, it could carry up to 4,000lbs of external stores and was also the first USAF fighter to have provision for air-to-air refuelling. A total of 4,457 Thunderjets were produced, of which no less than 3,025 were the F-84G variant, and the type was widely supplied to overseas and NATO countries under MDAP.

The instrument panel of the unarmed prototype XP-84 Thunderjet. For test purposes, a G-meter has been installed at top centre but this would be replaced by a gyro gunsight in production aircraft.

A publicity photo taken at Elgin AFB in 1953 showing an F-84E Thunderjet carrying a heavy ordnance load of two Tiny Tim 500lb warhead rocket bombs and twenty-four 5in HVAR (although the normal operational load would only be sixteen of the latter).

In 1950, one of the pre-production YP-84A prototypes was modified with cheek intakes replacing the usual nose intake.

In 1949, Republic proposed a swept-wing fighter based on the successful Thunderjet. To keep costs down, swept wings and tail surfaces were married to a standard F-84E fuselage and the Allison J35 engine was retained. In this form the prototype was designated YF-96A and first flew on June 1950, subsequently being redesignated YF-84F Thunderstreak.

As the results of German wartime research became available, Republic followed other manufacturers in looking to apply the benefits of swept wings. In 1949, the initial idea was to mate the new wings to a standard F-84E and in this form a prototype YF-96A flew on 3 June 1950. With the outbreak of the Korean War, new funds were made available but the USAF requested that the design be recast to use the more powerful Wright J65 engine (a licence-built version of the British Armstrong Siddeley Sapphire). Accommodating this required a redesign of the fuselage with a deeper air intake and consequently, much of the commonality with the F-84E was lost. Nevertheless, the aircraft was now renamed as the F-84F Thunderstreak and the first Sapphire-powered YF-84F flew on 14 February 1951, with deliveries of production aircraft commencing in January 1954 – too late for deployment in the Korean War. Total production was 3,431 aircraft, of which 715 were the RF-84F photo reconnaissance version, which featured wing-root intakes to allow installation of nose-mounted cameras. This first flew in February 1952 and it became operational in March 1954.

North American, producers of the famous Second World War P-51 Mustang, began looking at designs for a jet-propelled successor in 1944. Under the designation NA-140, this was a single-engined jet fighter similar to what was to become the FJ-1 Fury for the US Navy. However, the NA-140 featured a thinner wing and a slimmer fuselage. Power was to be provided by a single General Electric J35 axial-flow turbojet and the Air Force ordered three XP-86 prototypes in May 1945, wind tunnel testing indicating that performance would be as good as the rival Thunderjet. However, the North American team had become interested in the results of German research into swept wings and approval was given for the XP-86 design

With the outbreak of the Korean War the USAF became interested in a version of the F-84F powered by the much more powerful Wright J65 jet engine (a licence-built version of the Armstrong Siddeley Sapphire). Two J65-powered prototypes were followed by the definitive F-84F-RE production versions, the first of which (51-1346) is illustrated here. Note the extended cockpit canopy and dorsal spine.

The RF-84F Thunderflash was a photo reconnaissance version, which flew in prototype form in February 1952 but production aircraft only joined operational units from March 1954 onwards. Wing root intakes were adopted to allow for an extended nose housing a battery of cameras.

The first of three prototype XP-86s (45-59597 shown here) flew on 1 October 1947, and in the following year became the first US fighter to exceed Mach 1.

to be modified so that these could be incorporated. Work pressed ahead and the prototype XP-86 took to the air on 1 October 1947 as the world's first swept-wing single engine jet fighter, but only two months ahead of what was to be its great rival – the Russian Mig-15.

The prototype was still powered by the Allison J35-A-5 engine, rated at only 4,000lbs thrust, but it was capable of 618mph in level flight, and on 26 April 1948 it exceeded Mach 1 in a dive – the first US jet to do so. However, production F-86As had the more powerful General Electric J47, which offered 5,200lbs thrust, dramatically improving the aircraft's performance. Maximum speed was now 673mph at sea level and so thoughts turned to an attempt on the World Air Speed Record, which was then held by the US Navy with their Douglas Skystreak research aircraft at 650.796mph. On 15 September 1948, an F-86A set a new record of 670.981mph at low level over Muroc dry lake. Not only was the record broken by a substantial margin, but of greater significance was the fact that this was achieved by a standard production F-86A carrying normal operational equipment. The air force was naturally delighted with its new fighter, which was ordered in quantity and initially entered service in March 1949. It was at this time the name Sabre was officially adopted.

In 1949, the California-based 1st Fighter Group was one of the first to receive the new F-86A Sabre, and some of its aircraft are lined up in front of the control tower at March AFB.

The cockpit of an F-86A-5-NA Sabre, showing a bank of analogue instruments typical of the period. The only navigation aid is a standard radio compass (extreme left) but the A-1CM gunsight at top could also be used for aiming rockets or bombs.

A pair of F-86E Sabres belonging to the 56th Fighter Squadron, 33rd Fighter Wing, based at Otis AFB, Massachusetts during 1951. The F-86E was the second major production day fighter variant and entered service from March 1951 onwards.

The original Sabre design proved to be so good that only relatively minor changes were involved in subsequent production versions of the day fighter. From December 1950, the production switched to the F-86E, which featured a power-assisted all-flying tailplane to improve handling at transonic speeds. In 1952, production moved on the F-86F, which incorporated lessons learnt from experience in the Korean War. The most significant change was the introduction of the so-called '6-3' wing, in which the automatic wing slats were deleted and the wing leading edge extended 6 inches forward at the wing root tapering to a 3 inch extension at the tip. In addition, a more powerful J47-GE-27 turbojet rated at 5,910lb.s.t. was fitted. These changes made the Sabre better able to engage with the Mig-15s over Korea, which previously had a better performance at high altitudes and a better rate of turn.

In April 1953, North American flew the prototype F-86H, which differed visibly from earlier Sabres. Designed specifically for the fighter bomber role, it had an 8,920lb.s.t. General Electric J73 engine, which was larger and heavier than the J47, and this necessitated a deeper fuselage. Some 475 F-86H models were built and total US Sabre production reached 6,456. In addition, another 1,815 Sabres were built under licence by Canadair, of which 428 were supplied to the RAF and 300 were built by Mitsubishi in Japan. The total US figure includes the radar-equipped F-86D/K interceptor, which is described separately.

The F-86F first flew in March 1952 and had a more powerful General Electric J47-GE-27 engine, which boosted top speed to 688mph at sea level. The first batches of F-86Fs retained wing leading edge slats but North American engineers developed the so-called '6–3' wing, which markedly improved manoeuvrability and was fitted to all subsequent production aircraft with conversion kits supplied for the earlier F models.

The ultimate day fighter version of the Sabre was the F-86H, which had the much more powerful General Electric J73-GE-3 engine, necessitating a wider intake and deeper fuselage. Wingspan was increased by 2 feet and the landing gear was strengthened to cope with an increased gross 21,800lb gross weight. First flown in September 1953, it entered service in late 1954 and was used mainly in the fighter bomber role, being one of the first USAF fighters equipped to carry tactical nuclear weapons.

The Sabre was widely exported to NATO and other friendly allied countries. This is one of over 300 ex-USAF F-86F Sabres supplied to the Chinese Nationalist Air Force based on Taiwan. The first few were delivered in November 1954, but in 1958, Nationalist Sabres, now armed with Sidewinder missiles, claimed twenty-nine Migs in aerial engagements with Chinese Communist forces.

In 1950, with the F-86 now rolling off the production lines North American began looking at an advanced successor. Air force interest resulted in an order for two YF-100A prototypes and thirty-two production aircraft. The first prototype flew on 25 May 1953 and was powered by a 9,700lb.s.t. (14,800lb with afterburning) Pratt & Whitney J57 turbojet. This endowed the F-100 with a remarkable performance and it was the first combat aircraft capable of exceeding Mach 1 in level flight. The F-100A Super Sabre became fully operational in September 1954 and eventually a total of 2,294 F-100s were delivered.

Unlike the United Kingdom, the United States was not vulnerable to attack by land-based bombers during the Second World War and consequently, a viable air defence system was unnecessary and virtually non-existent. This situation changed with the onset of the Cold War and the threat of attack by Soviet bombers armed with nuclear weapons. The only purpose-built American radar-equipped night fighter produced during the Second World War was the twin-boom Northrop P-61 Black Widow. It was natural that the company would consider producing a jet-propelled successor and a contract for two XP-89 prototypes was awarded in December 1946. The design was unadventurous, with a shoulder-mounted straight wing and two Allison J35 engines in the lower half of the fuselage. The two crew were seated in tandem under a continuous cockpit canopy and all but the first prototype had large fixed wing tip fuel tanks. A heavy armament of six 20mm cannon was mounted in the nose. Making its first flight from Edwards AFB on 16 August 1948, the prototype (now designated XF-89A Scorpion) was subsequently lost in a crash in February 1950. Nevertheless, production F-89As became operational in mid-1951 and production continued with F-89B and C models, which featured

The supersonic North American F-100 Super Sabre was originally known as the Sabre 45 as it was a development of the earlier aircraft with a 45° swept wing and a more powerful Pratt & Whitney J57 engine. Two YF-100 prototypes were ordered in 1952, and the first of these flew on 25 May 1953. The Super Sabre entered service with the 479th Day Fighter Wing in 1954, and subsequently 2,294 F-100s of all variants were produced up to 1959.

This air-to-air shot of the first YF-100 ((52-574) clearly shows the clean lines and sharply swept wing of the Super Sabre. This aircraft set a World Air Speed Record of 755.149mph on 29 October 1953, but in August 1955, a production F-100C set a new record of 822,135mph, the first in excess of Mach 1.

equipment changes and progressively more powerful J35 engines. However, all F-89s were grounded for a period in 1952 following accidents caused by structural failures, which required some changes to the wing design before operations could be resumed. A total of 1,052 Scorpions were produced but over half of these were the F-89D, in which the guns were removed and replaced by a total of 104 2.75in FFAR carried in pods mounted on the front of the wing tip tanks. The F-89D became operational in 1954 and was later followed by the F-89H, in which the wing tip pods were each modified to carry three Hughes Falcon air-to-air guided missiles as well as twenty-one FFAR, although this version did not enter service until 1956 and was followed in 1957 by the F-89J, a conversion of the F-89D with provision for the Douglas MB-1 Genie unguided nuclear-tipped rocket.

In the wake of the Berlin Airlift and the consequent deepening of the Cold War there was some urgency to strengthening America's air defences and the USAF therefore looked for an interim jet all-weather fighter to supplement the F-89 Scorpion. Responding to an air force request, Lockheed looked at modifying the successful T-33 (then still designated TF-80) trainer for this role. This proved to be relatively straightforward, with the radar equipment mounted in a modified nose and the operator seated in the second seat behind the pilot. To boost performance an afterburner was to be installed in the rear fuselage. These changes resulted

The Northrop F-89 Scorpion was the USAF's first purpose designed all-weather jet fighter. Shown here in an overall black livery is the prototype XF-89, which flew on 16 August 1948, but was subsequently lost in an accident on 22 February 1950.

The second prototype, designated YF-89A, flew in November 1949 and retained the standard natural metal finish. Also apparent in this view is the lengthened and more pointed nose, which was representative of production aircraft.

A line-up of F-89C Scorpions in 1952 awaiting delivery to the 74th Fighter Interceptor Squadron. Standard armament at this time comprised six nose-mounted 20mm cannon, and provision for two 1,600lb bombs and up to sixteen HVAR 5in rockets.

The F-89D entered service in 1954 and introduced a major change in armament. The 20mm cannon were removed and new wing tip pods each carried no less than fifty-two 2.75in folding-fin air rockets (FFAR). The aircraft shown here is actually an F-89B modified to act as the YF-89D prototype.

A potential rival to the Northrop F-89 was the Curtiss XP-87 Blackhawk, which flew in prototype form on 5 March 1948. For a two-seat fighter it was unusually large and heavy, and was powered by no less than four J34 engines. Armament was originally planned as four 0.5in machine guns in nose and tail-mounted automatic turrets, but this was changed to a more conventional four forward-firing 20mm cannon. Following encouraging test flight results orders were placed for fifty-seven F-87A fighters and thirty RF-87A photo reconnaissance versions.

A head-on view of the XP-87 prototype showing the disposition of the four 3,000lb.s.t. Westinghouse J34 engines. However, production aircraft would be powered by two 5,200lb.s.t. General Electric J47 engines. In the event, production orders were cancelled in favour of the Northrop Scorpion, forcing the Curtiss Wright Corporation to cease aircraft production.

The F-94 Starfire was produced as an interim jet-powered, all-weather fighter by the simple expedient of adapting the existing T-33 two-seat trainer version of the F-80 shooting Star. Modified by the addition of a nose-mounted APG-32 radar with the operator occupying the rear seat, it first flew in this form on 16 April 1949.

Its proximity to the Soviet Union made Alaska particularly vulnerable to attack, and consequently, some of the first squadrons to receive the F-94A were located there. This example belonging to the 449 FIS is shown at Ladd AFB, Alaska, in the winter of 1952. Note the fuel tanks located under the wing tips – a distinguishing feature of this variant.

The pilot's cockpit of the F-94A is dominated by the radar repeater screen at centre. Although an interception would be controlled by the rear seat radar operator, the repeater improved the pilot's situational awareness, particularly in the closing stages of the interception.

This F-94B Starfire of the Japan-based 35th Fighter Wing is pictured in September 1951, during the time of the Korean War. Note the tip tanks now positioned on the wing centreline.

The ultimate Starfire variant was the F-94C, which first flew in 1950 and incorporated several significant changes, including a new power plant in the form of an 8,7650lb.s.t. Pratt & Whitney J48 engine (licence-produced Rolls-Royce Tay), which considerably boosted performance. Other changes included a new thinner wing, swept tailplane, and a new all-rocket armament of twenty-four 2.75in FFAR clustered in the nose around the radome for the APG-40 radar. Later modifications included pods mounted on the wing leading edges, each containing an additional twelve rockets.

The ancestry of the Starfire is clearly illustrated in this view of an F-80C Shooting Star acting as chase plane for an early production F-94C.

in the F-94 Starfire, and the first of two YF-94s (both converted TF-80s) flew on 16 April 1949. Production F-94As reached service squadrons in May 1950 – the USAF's first jet-powered, all-weather fighter. The next version was the F-94B, which could be distinguished by its tip tanks centred on the wing rather than underslung as on the F-80 and F-94A. However, the F-94C, which entered service in 1953, was a much more fundamental redesign to the extent that it was initially allocated a new type designation as the F-97. Compared to the F-94A/B, which had a maximum speed of 606mph, the F-94C was faster at 640mph and had a significantly better initial rate of climb (almost 8,000ft/min). The F-94C remained in service until 1959, the earlier versions having been replaced by 1954.

Up to around 1950 it was always considered that an all-weather fighter had to carry a navigator/observer to operate the radar system and provide guidance for the pilot. However, advances in electronics were reaching the point where a workable airborne interception system could be monitored and operated by a single pilot without the need for a second crew member. To take advantage of this, in 1949, North American proposed a radar-equipped version of its F-86 Sabre single-seat fighter. A letter of intent for two YF-86D prototypes was issued in October 1949, some urgency being apparent in the wake of the news that the Russians had successfully tested their first atomic bomb.

As built, the F-86D differed from the standard Sabre in several respects and again was initially given a separate designation as the F-95A, but for political and accounting reasons it reverted to its original designation. The most obvious difference was the addition of a

A single-seat, all-weather variant of the North American F-86 Sabre was initially ordered as the YF-95A but by the time the prototype flew on 22 December 1949, it had been redesignated as the YF-86D. The radome above the air intake housed an AN/APG-36 radar, which was coupled to a Hughes E-3 or E-4 fire control system. This combination partly automated the interception process so that it could be handled by the pilot alone without assistance from a radar operator as in the F-89 or F-94 all-weather fighters.

prominent radome above the lowered air intake. A clamshell cockpit canopy was fitted for easier jettisoning in the event of the ejector seat being used and the J47 jet engine was equipped with an afterburner. The gun armament was replaced by a battery of twenty-four FFAR unguided rockets housed in an under-fuselage retractable tray. Standard Sabre wings and undercarriage were retained but a new power-operated, all-flying tailplane was fitted. In addition, General Electric developed an electronic fuel control system that reduced pilot workload and simplified operation of the afterburner. Whilst such equipment is very common and reliable in this digital age, in the early 1950s it relied on valve technology and experienced numerous problems before it could be made to work reliably. Consequently, although the first YF-86D flew on 22 December 1949, it was not until April 1954 that the Sabre Dog (as it was affectionately known) became fully operational. From 1956 to 1960, many Dogs were converted to F-86L standards by an upgrade of the avionic systems and installation of a SAGE compatible air-ground data link. In addition, the F-86K was a variant in which the rocket armament was replaced by four 20mm cannon, these being intended for NATO air forces, including 221 assembled by Fiat in Italy.

An Air Force requirement for a long-range penetration/escort fighter brought out some interesting ideas. Mention has already been made of the Bell XP-83, and in June 1949, Lockheed flew the first of two XF-90 experimental fighters. It was an attractive swept-wing

The addition of the radome improved the Sabre's aerodynamics and this, together with the addition of an afterburner for the J47 engine, meant that the F-86D was actually the fastest Sabre variant. This was clearly illustrated on 16 July 1953, when the F-86D shown here (51-2945) was piloted by Lieutenant Colonel William Barnes to a new World Air Speed Record of 715.697mph.

The F-86D was the first US fighter to carry an all-rocket armament. This consisted of a retractable pack carrying twenty-four 2.75in Mighty Mouse FFAR. Although the D variant began to roll off North American's production lines in 1951, the type did not reach Air Defence Command units until the summer of 1953 due to delays in delivery of engines and the complex fire control equipment.

Another variant of the Sabre was the YF-93A, which flew on 25 January 1950. Originally known as the F-86C, it was intended as a long-range escort fighter and was powered by a Pratt & Whitney J48 centrifugal-flow jet engine. As this had a greater diameter than the standard axial-flow J47, the fuselage was redesigned and it was fed by lateral air intakes to allow for a radar installation in the nose. A heavy armament of six 20mm cannon was carried and twin main wheels were fitted on the undercarriage to cope with the substantially increased weight of this version. However, production contracts were cancelled in January 1949 and the two prototypes were subsequently used for research purposes.

fighter powered by two Westinghouse J34-WE-11 turbojets rated at 3,600lb.s.t. (4,200lb with afterburning) but with a maximum all-up weight of 26,000lbs, much of which was fuel for an estimated range of 2,300 miles, it was seriously underpowered. Although the flight test programme was completed without serious problems, the XF-90A offered no advantages over existing aircraft such as the F-86 Sabre and the programme was halted.

Another factor in the XF-90's demise was the existence of a rival aircraft in the form of the McDonnell XF-88 Voodoo, which had been designed to the same specification and was also powered by two Westinghouse J34 engines. The first of two prototypes was flown on 20 October 1948 and demonstrated a top speed of 641mph. The second XF-88 was fitted with an afterburner system developed by McDonnell, and this aircraft was capable of almost 700mph at sea level and could climb to 30,000 feet in four minutes. In testing against the Lockheed XF-90 (and also the North American XF-93A) carried out in 1951, the XF-88 was adjudged the winner, but at the time production priority was accorded to existing types and the penetration fighter project was shelved.

Experience in the Korean War prompted a revival of the long-range fighter, this time specifically to escort the new Convair B-36 bombers. McDonnell proposed an enlarged version of the XF-88, which was to be powered by two Pratt & Whitney J57 turbojets. The

The Lockheed XF-90 resulted from the 1946 requirement for a long-range escort fighter and first flew in June 1949. Like the rival XF-88, it was powered by a pair of afterburning Westinghouse J34 jet engines but its performance was unexceptional and further development was cancelled in 1950.

The XF-90 was an attractive looking aircraft and a noticeable feature was the pair of jettisonable wing tip tanks, which enabled the aircraft to attain a range in excess of 2,300 miles.

The McDonnell XF-88 Voodoo was another of several competing designs resulting from the USAF requirement for a long-range escort or penetration fighter. First flown on 20 October 1948, it featured a very thin swept wing, whose span was considerably less than the overall length of the aircraft.

The second XF-88 had more powerful Westinghouse J34 engines, boosted by the addition of short afterburners. Although the Voodoo was preferred over the Lockheed XF-90 and North American XF-93, a change of priorities and lack of funding led to the programme being cancelled in 1950.

Despite a lack of production orders, the two XF-88 prototypes continued to provide valuable data in the development of high-speed fighters, and in 1953, the first prototype was modified as a test bed for the Allison T38 turboprop. This was installed in the nose, and the two J34 jet engines were retained. In this configuration it was redesignated XF-88B and subsequently became the first propeller-equipped aircraft to exceed Mach 1 (albeit by a small margin). *via Aviation Archives*

In 1951, the USAF issued a revised requirement for a long-range escort fighter, which was met by adapting and improving the earlier XF-88. The fuselage was lengthened by over 13 feet and power was provided by a pair of 10,000lb.s.t. Pratt & Whitney J57 engines, almost tripling the installed dry thrust and boosting maximum speed to over 1,000mph. This formed the basis for the F-101 Voodoo, which flew on 29 September 1954, although by then the long-range escort fighter role had been cancelled but the Voodoo was subsequently produced in quantity as a tactical and reconnaissance fighter, and as a two-seat, all-weather interceptor.

new design became the F-101 Voodoo and first flew on 29 September 1954, by which time it had also been adapted for the nuclear strike role. While outside the scope of this book, a two-seat interceptor version F-101B was developed in the late 1950s, and in total, 807 Voodoos of all variants were produced from 1954 to 1962.

As far back as 1945, the air force had requested proposals for a jet interceptor capable of 700mph and able to reach 50,000 feet in four minutes. Convair initially proposed a ramjet-powered, delta-wing design based on the wartime work of the German engineer Dr Alexander Lippisch. Originally ordered as the XP-92, it was redesignated as the XP-92A with a conventional J33 jet engine installed after the ramjet was deemed impractical. Making its first flight on 18 September 1948, the XP-92A was used purely for research into delta wings. However, in May 1949, the air force asked for proposals for an integrated weapons system in which a new supersonic airframe would be designed around the Hughes MA-1 fire control system and its associated Falcon air-to-air missile. This was the first time that the weapons system approach had been applied to a new military aircraft. Convair proposed a scaled-up version of their XP-92A, which received the designation F-102A, and the first YF-102 flew on 24 October 1953 but was destroyed in an accident only nine days later. The second YF-102A flew on 11 January 1954, but testing quickly revealed the fact that despite having a 14,500lb.s.t Pratt & Whitney J57 engine, the aircraft was unable to exceed Mach 1. Fortunately it was around this time that the concept of area rule to reduce transonic drag came to prominence and the YF-102A was rebuilt to incorporate this feature. The fuselage was lengthened by 11 feet and was waisted around mid chord of the wing, whilst aerodynamic bulges known as 'Whitcomb bodies' were incorporated into the rear fuselage. Thus modified, the first of four new YF-102As flew on 20 December 1954, and on the following day exceeded

In the immediate post-war period, Convair went ahead with the concept of a ramjet interceptor. However, the ramjet proved impractical and the resulting XF-92A was powered by an Allison J33 turbojet. In this form it first flew on 18 September 1948, and was the world's first delta-winged jet aircraft.

By the time that the XF-92A was flown, it was no longer regarded as a potential fighter but was used extensively to investigate the characteristics of the novel delta-wing design until it was retired following a ground accident in October 1953.

Mach 1 in the climb. However, the definitive F-102A Delta Dagger did not become operational until 1956, and its subsequent career lies outside the scope of this book.

The progress made in jet fighter performance from 1944 to 1954 is no more clearly demonstrated than by a spectacular aircraft that first flew in prototype form on 4 March 1954. This was the Lockheed F-104 Starfighter, at that time dubbed as the 'missile with a man in it'! A long, thin fuselage housed a single Wright XJ65 with afterburner, and a pair of incredibly small and thin wings was attached. Production aircraft had a General Electric J79 engine and the Starfighter was the first operational fighter capable of flying at twice the speed of sound – something that would have been unthinkable only a few years earlier.

The YF-102 was basically a scaled-up XF-92A with a more powerful Pratt & Whitney J57 turbojet and was expected to be capable of supersonic speeds. However, tests with the first YF-102, which flew on 24 October 1953, quickly revealed that the aircraft was stubbornly subsonic.

The first redesigned YF-102A flew on 20 December 1954. The most obvious change was the lengthened fuselage, which was waisted in order to conform with the new area rule theory, and this enabled the aircraft to exceed Mach 1 in level flight. The production F-102A Delta Dagger was the USAF's first aircraft designed as an integral part of a weapon system (WS201A), which also included the Hughes MG-3 fire control system, the Falcon AAM, and built-in links with Air Defence Command's SAGE system. The F-102 did not enter service until 1956, but subsequently equipped twenty-six interceptor squadrons by 1958.

By the end of the decade reviewed by this book, prototypes of revolutionary aircraft such as the Lockheed XF-104 Starfighter were offering speeds well in excess of 1,000mph. *PRM Aviation Collection*

Chapter Four

United States Navy Jet Fighters

In the US Navy responsibility for the preparation of specifications and requests for proposals for naval aircraft rested with the Bureau of Aeronautics (BuAer), which began investigating jet propulsion as early as 1942. Although considering mixed-power designs, it also approached the young McDonnell company to design their first pure jet fighter. Design of what was to become the FD-1 Phantom was hampered by the fact that detailed specifications of the Westinghouse engines were not available until a relatively late stage and various combinations of two, four or even eight engines (each of a different size and thrust rating) were considered before a twin-engined layout was finalised around a pair of Westinghouse W19-XB-2B turbojets (later redesignated J30 and producing 1,600lb.s.t. in production versions). The FD-1 was a relatively simple but clean design with straight wings and tail unit, a tricycle undercarriage and the engines buried in the wing roots. The first flight was delayed due to issues with engine deliveries but eventually occurred on 26 January 1945. The test programme

The US Navy's first jet fighter was the McDonnell Phantom, of which the prototype XFD-1 (48235) shown here was flown on 26 January 1945. *via Aviation Archives*

The second prototype Phantom (48326) became the first US pure jet aircraft to land on an aircraft carrier during trials aboard the USS *Franklin D. Roosevelt* (CV42) on 21 July 1946, when the XFD-1 also demonstrated the ability to make a free take-off unaided by a catapult, albeit in brisk wind conditions. *via Aviation Archives*

As from 28 August 1947, the Phantom was redesignated FH-1, and by that time the first operational squadron, VF-17A, had begun receiving production aircraft. In May 1948, the squadron completed carrier qualification, three years before the Royal Navy's Attackers achieved similar status. Some of the squadron's Phantoms are shown aboard the USS *Franklin D. Roosevelt*.

An FD-1 Phantom of VF-17A makes a catapult launch from the USS *Saipan* (CVL48) during carrier qualification training. The unit was never deployed as a front-line operational squadron due to the Phantom's limited range and endurance, but nevertheless, much valuable experience in the operation of jets aboard carriers was gained. *via Aviation Archives*

The advent of the new jets meant that they were the centre of attention wherever they went. In this instance, a pair of FD-1 Phantoms belonging to VMF122 are closely inspected by officers and men at Jacksonville NAS in 1948. *via Aviation Archives*

was not without incident as the prototype was destroyed in a crash and the second XFD-1 damaged in a wheels-up landing. Nevertheless, the navy ordered 100 FD-1 Phantoms in March 1945, although this was subsequently reduced to sixty in the post-war period. Production aircraft were delivered from January 1947 until May 1948, at which point the designation was changed to FH-1 to avoid possible confusion with projected Douglas jet fighters whose company identifier was also D. Subsequently the Phantom was replaced in front-line service as early as 1949, although it remained active in a training role until 1953.

Following on from the Phantom, the F2H Banshee flew in prototype form on 11 January 1947 and was very similar in outline to the FH-1, but larger and heavier. Nevertheless, the extra power resulted in improved performance with maximum speed raised from 479mph to 532mph, and service ceiling from 41,000 feet to almost 45,000 feet. There was almost a 50 per cent increase in range to 1,475 statute miles due to the use of fixed-wing tip tanks. The Banshee entered service in 1949 as a daytime interceptor and fighter/bomber but in 1950, the radar-equipped F2H-2N was introduced. The subsequent -3 and -4 variants were similar but with improved radars. There was also a photographic reconnaissance version, the F2H-2P, the US Navy's first jet in this role. The Banshee was also the navy's first jet all-weather fighter and in 1949 featured in the first use of an ejector seat by a US pilot in an emergency situation. It was also notable for its high altitude performance and on one occasion, an F2H-1 is recorded to have reached 52,000 feet. In all, 895 Banshees were delivered and in 1955, thirty-nine were

Even while the prototype Phantom was under development, the US Navy authorised McDonnell to proceed with the design of a larger and more powerful fighter, which was initially designated XF2D-1 and named Banshee. The first of three prototypes flew on 11 January 1947, and was powered by two 3,000lb.s.t. Westinghouse J34-WE-22 engines. The family resemblance to the earlier Phantom is clearly shown in this view of the second XF2D-1 ((99859). *via Aviation Archives*

Production Banshees were designated F2H-1, and deliveries to VF-171 began in March 1949. One of their aircraft is shown aboard the USS *Franklin D. Roosevelt* (CV42) during NATO Exercise Mainbrace in 1952. Tail code R indicates Carrier Air Group 17 (CVG17). *via Aviation Archives*

The F2H-2 Banshee, which flew in August 1949, featured a lengthened fuselage and fixed-wing tip tanks, which substantially increased fuel capacity, and to cope with the additional weight, more powerful 3,250lb.s.t. J34-WE-34 engines were installed. This photo was taken in 1954 and shows a line-up of F2H-2s belonging to VF12 assigned to Carrier Air Group 1. *via Aviation Archives*

The Banshee was widely used during the Korean War and this pair of F2H-2s from Carrier Air Wing 4 is providing cover for Task Force 77 steaming off the Korean Coast at the end of hostilities in July 1953. The US Navy generally preferred the Banshee over the contemporary Grumman Panther due to its twin-engine reliability and greater range, but it was significantly more expensive, which limited the numbers that could be ordered.

A few F2H-2N radar-equipped, single-seat night fighter versions of the Banshee were produced, the first flying in February 1950. This formed the basis of the F2H-3, in which the fuselage was again lengthened to increase fuel capacity and no less than 250 of this variant were produced. The final production version was the F2H-4 shown here, which had the more powerful 3,600lb.s.t. J34-WE-38 engines as well as a Hughes AN/APG-37 radar, and entered service from September 1953. *via Aviation Archives*

A photo reconnaissance version of the Banshee was designated F2H-2P, and the first of fifty-eight examples flew in October 1950. They could be distinguished by the lengthened nose, which held a battery of cameras, as shown in this line-up of VMP-62 aircraft aboard USS *Franklin D. Roosevelt* in 1955. *via Aviation Archives*

The US Navy did not start receiving production FD-1 Phantoms until the summer of 1947, but in the meantime there was an urgent need for its pilots to gain jet experience. Consequently, three Lockheed P-80 Shooting Stars were transferred to the navy in June 1945 for that purpose but retained their air force serial numbers and type designation (the first aircraft 29667 is shown here). One of these was fitted with an arrestor hook for carrier trials carried out aboard the USS *Franklin D. Roosevelt* in November 1946, during the course of which it became the first jet aircraft to be catapult-launched from a carrier.

In 1948, the US Navy obtained another fifty F-80C Shooting Stars for use as advanced jet trainers. In service these were designated TO-1 (later TV-1) and one of several based at NAS North Island, California, is shown here. The success of the Lockheed jet in the training role subsequently led to orders for 699 two-seat TO-2s, the navy equivalent of the air force's T-33.

transferred to the Royal Canadian Navy, who flew them until 1962, although the US Navy withdrew them from front-line service in 1959.

In September 1944, BuAer had set a competition for a new single-engined jet fighter, which resulted in two companies – North American and Chance Vought – being awarded contracts to build prototypes. The first to fly, on 2 October 1946, was the Chance Vought XF6U-1 Pirate, which was powered by a 3,000lb.s.t. Westinghouse J34 turbojet. Apart from three prototypes, a further thirty F6U-1s were delivered in 1949–50; they featured aerodynamic changes to improve directional stability and were fitted with an afterburner system that boosted thrust to 4,200lbs. However, the afterburner proved to be very unreliable and without it performance was mediocre to say the least, and so the production aircraft were never issued to an operational unit.

North American's offering was the NA-134, which was subsequently ordered as the FJ-1 Fury and was powered by the General Electric J35, producing 4,000lb.s.t. This was the first US jet fighter to utilise a nose intake and ducting was routed below the cockpit, whilst the provision of fuel tanks in the fuselage resulted in a distinctive deep profile. The first of three XFJ-1 prototypes flew on 27 November 1946, but original orders for 100 aircraft were cut back to thirty and it only briefly equipped one operational squadron (VF-5A) from 1948 to

Vought was eager to produce a jet-age successor to the wartime F4U Corsair and the result was the Vought F6U Pirate, which flew in prototype form on 2 October 1946. The three XF6U-1s were all powered by a single 3,000lb.s.t. Westinghouse J34-WE-22, but the thirty production F6U-1 Pirates were fitted with an afterburner, the first such application in a US Navy fighter, which increased thrust to 4,225lb.s.t.

This view of an F6U-1 shows the straight wing with air intakes at the root while the long nose provides room for the pilot and an armament of four 20mm cannon. However, performance was disappointing and the afterburner proved to be temperamental and unreliable. Consequently, the Pirate was never used operationally and further development was cancelled.

Produced in response to a US Navy 1944 requirement was the North American FJ-1 Fury. The Company made extensive use of its experience gained with the P-51 Mustang in designing the Fury, which utilised the wing and tail surfaces of the Mustang married to a new, rather tubby fuselage. The prototype XFJ-1 Fury flew on 11 September 1946, and the first of thirty production aircraft were delivered from March 1948. Photo shows the third prototype (39055) fitted with wing tip fuel tanks.

Production Furies were powered by a 4,000lb.s.t. Allison J35 engine, giving a maximum speed of 547mph at 9,000 feet. The FJ-1 only equipped one fighter squadron VF-5A (later VF-51), which subsequently became the first jet fighter squadron to form part of an operational Carrier Air Group (CVG-5), aboard USS *Boxer* (CV21) in 1948/49.

The FJ-1 Fury only served with VF-5A for fourteen months before being replaced by newer types. However, the aircraft were then utilised by Naval Air Reserve units, as illustrated by this neat formation of the Oakland Naval Air Reserve in 1951.

The early jets had a relatively poor take-off performance and needed a long flight deck. Consequently, much of the early tests and trials were carried out aboard the US Navy's largest carriers available at the time. These were the three Midway class completed after the Second World War and originally designed to accommodate up to 130 piston-engined fighters and attack aircraft. This view of USS *Coral Sea* (CV43) in 1948 gives some idea of her size.

The wartime Essex class carriers proved surprisingly adaptable in the jet age. Initially, eight of the class were modified under a scheme known as SCB-27A, which included substantially increased aviation fuel stowage and improved aircrew facilities. Progressive modifications to operate the ever larger and heavier jets eventually resulted in ships modified to SCB-125 standard, which incorporated an angled deck, steam catapults and a mirror landing sight. In 1953, the Essex class carrier USS *Antietam* (CV36) was the first to incorporate the British concept of an angled deck and the success of trials led to its widespread adoption.

late 1949. Maximum speed was 547mph but service ceiling was only 32,000 feet. At this point it is worth noting that a swept-wing version with a slimmer fuselage was adopted by the air force and became the famous F-86 Sabre.

The performance of both the Fury and the Pirate fell below navy requirements but something better was in prospect in the shape of the Grumman F9F-2 Panther. Grumman had started development of a jet fighter under the designation G-79 and had considered various engine options before choosing the British Rolls-Royce Nene, which at 5,000lb.s.t. was the most powerful turbojet available. BuAer agreed with this proposal but arranged for the engine to be produced under licence by Pratt & Whitney as the J42. The first of three prototype XF9F-2s flew on 24 August 1947, and by May 1949, the Panther was in large-scale production and was entering service. The F9F-3 and -4 variants were to be powered by the Allison J33 rated at 4,600lb.s.t. but most of these were re-engined with the J42 or the contracts reallocated to the F9F-5, which was the final Panther variant and the one produced in the greatest numbers. This was powered by a developed version of the J42 (Nene) known as the J48 (Tay), which offered an increased thrust rating of 6,250lb increasing maximum level speed to 604mph, although due to increased weight the F9F-5 showed no improvement in rate of climb and service ceiling. Some 1,387 Panthers were produced and the type played a prominent role in the Korean War, equipping no less than twenty-four US Navy and Marine Corps squadrons.

By the time the Korean War started in 1950, the US Navy's standard jet fighter was the Grumman F9F Panther. The original XF9F-1 was a Grumman design for a night fighter powered by four Westinghouse J30 engines, but this idea was abandoned and a more conventional single-engined day fighter resulted under the designation XF9F-2. The prototype flew on 24 November 1947, and deliveries of production F9F-2s began in 1949. One of these is shown preparing for take-off from the USS *Midway* (CVB41) in 1952.

In response to a navy desire to have an alternative engine supplier, Grumman produced the F9F-3, which was powered by a 4,600lb.s.t. Allison J33 engine, and the first of these flew in August 1948. An early production example is shown here in the markings of the Naval Air Test Centre based at Patuxent River NAS in July 1950. However, the Allison-engined version proved less successful than hoped and the fifty-four F9F-3s ordered were subsequently converted to F9F-2 standard.

The ultimate version of the Panther was the F9F-5, which was powered by a 6,250lb.s.t. Pratt & Whitney J48, an improved version of the J42/Nene, and could be identified by a taller fin and a 2ft fuselage extension. First flown in December 1949, the F9F-5 became the major production version, with over 600 being built. The example shown here is involved in angled deck trials aboard USS *Antietam* in 1953.

The Grumman Panther was widely deployed by the US Navy during the Korean War. This F9F-2 belongs to Reserve Squadron VF-721, which was embarked on the USS *Boxer* (CV21) from March to October 1951. Despite being outperformed by the swept-wing Mig-15, Panthers managed to shoot down no less than seven Migs during the war, although two Panthers were lost. The destruction of a Mig-15 by a Panther of VF-111 was claimed as the first ever successful jet versus jet combat.

Flight deck activity aboard USS *Boxer* in 1951 as it recovers a section of Panthers. An F9F-2 Panther of VF-721 has just landed and the deck handlers are disengaging the arrester hook while another Panther makes a go-around as the deck is occupied. In the distance a third aircraft can be seen turning in towards the carrier in preparation for landing.

The appearance of the Mig-15 at the start of the Korean War suddenly highlighted the need for a swept-wing jet fighter. Three Panthers modified by the incorporation of a 35° swept wing were ordered in March 1951 and the first of these flew only six months later in November 1951, by which time the name Cougar had been adopted, but it retained the F9F designation, becoming the F9F-6. After testing and evaluation, squadron deliveries commenced in November 1952, and eventually a total of 1,988 Cougars were delivered, including 712 improved F9F-8 variants and 399 two-seat F9F-8T trainers.

The sudden need to bring high performance swept-wing fighters into service also resulted in the navy looking at the possibility of a naval version of the air force's very successful F-86 Sabre. North American's response (NA181) was accepted and an order for three prototype FJ-2 Furies was placed in March 1951. In order to reduce development time, these incorporated only minimal changes to the F-86E airframe to adapt it for naval trials. The standard 5,200lb.s.t. J47 was retained and the first XFJ-2 flew on 27 December 1951, and two aircraft completed carrier qualification trails twelve months later. The production FJ-2 Fury featured folding wings, AN/APG-30 gunnery radar, a wider track undercarriage and an uprated 6,000lb.s.t. J47-GE-2 turbojet. Top speed was 676mph at sea level and initial rate of climb a

Although Grumman had investigated a swept-wing version of the F9F as early as 1947, there were doubts about the suitability of swept-wing fighters for carrier operations due to their handling problems at low speeds. However, the appearance of Mig-15s over Korea resulted in a change of policy and three swept-wing XF9F-6s were ordered in December 1950. The name Cougar was adopted and the first prototype, shown here, flew in September 1951.

Despite the high priority accorded to development of the F9F-6 Cougar, it was not until November 1952 that production aircraft began to reach naval squadrons, and by the time they were ready for operational service, the Korean War was over. Nevertheless, a total of 1,988 Cougar variants were produced and it was widely deployed by navy and marine squadrons for more than a decade. This image shows a line-up of aircraft belonging to VF-153 aircraft aboard USS *Yorktown* (CV10) in September 1954.

F9F-6 Cougars of VF-51 and VF-153 move forward in preparation for catapult launches from USS *Yorktown*, September 1954. The aircraft in the foreground clearly shows the wing fences and leading edge slats, which were introduced to improve the low speed handling characteristics of this swept-wing fighter.

The final single-seat version of the Cougar was the F9F-8, which first flew on 18 December 1953 (later two-seat trainer version was the F9F-8T). This retained the 7,250lb.s.t. Pratt & Whitney J48-P-8 engine but introduced various aerodynamic refinements. The example shown here is carrying out tests with the AIM-9 Sidewinder AAM in 1955. This highly successful missile, originally developed by the US Navy, became operational with F9F-8 Cougar squadrons in 1956.

The first two XFJ-2 Furies were basically F-86E Sabres modified by the addition of an arrester hook, lengthened nose wheel leg and catapult attachment points. One of these is aboard USS *Coral Sea* (CVA43) while carrying out carrier trails in December 1952.

Production FJ-2 Furies featured hydraulically folding wings and were armed with four 20mm cannon instead of the hitherto traditional fighter armament of six 0.5in machine guns. Almost all of the 200 FJ-2s delivered by September 1954 were allocated to marine squadrons, the first being VMF-122 in January 1954.

respectable 7,230ft/min. Production of the FJ-2 was slow due to the priority given to supplying F-86 Sabres to the air force and consequently, only twenty-five Furies had been delivered by the end of 1953. From January 1954, the FJ-2 was allocated to USMC (United States Marine Corps) fighter squadrons.

A prototype of the FJ-3 with the more powerful 7,800lb.s.t. Wright J65-W-2 (Sapphire) was flown in on 3 July 1953 and this version entered service with VF-173 in September 1954, subsequently equipping seventeen naval and four marine fighter squadrons. Visually FJ-3 could be identified by the wider nose intake required by the J65 engine. Final Fury variant was the FJ-4, in which the main changes were a reprofiled fuselage to provide more space for internal fuel and a new thinner wing. First flown on 28 October 1954, the FJ-4 served only with marine units and did not enter service until 1956. Fury production totalled 1,115 of all variants, the last being delivered in 1958.

Whilst the Fury and Cougar were adaptations of existing aircraft, the navy had previously sponsored development of a swept-wing fighter. This led Grumman to offer several design iterations, which started with swept wings and then progressed to a delta-winged project, but in each case there was considerable doubt about the low speed characteristics of such aircraft. Nevertheless, two XF10F-1 Jaguar prototypes were ordered in April 1948, but by 1951 the design had been completely altered to incorporate a variable geometry wing that could change sweep angle from 13.5° to 42.5°. In addition, the wing central pivot point moved fore and aft as the angle of sweep was changed. Powered by a Westinghouse J40, which was expected to provide 7,310lb.s.t. (10,900lb with afterburning), maximum speed was estimated at 710mph and

The FJ-2 was not considered suitable for carrier operations but the subsequent FJ-3, powered by a 7,700lb.s.t. J65-W-16A engine, which first flew on 3 July 1953, began to reach navy squadrons in mid-1954. This view shows a line-up of FJ-3 Furies allocated to VC-3 for operational testing at Moffat Field, California.

The FJ-3 was the major production version of the Fury, some 538 being produced. In 1956, around eighty of these were modified as FJ-3Ms equipped to carry the Sidewinder AAM. This is an FJ-3M of VF-211 aboard the USS *Bon Homme Richard* (CV31) in August 1956.

Development of the very advanced Grumman XF10F-1 Jaguar variable geometry jet fighter began in the late 1940s and the sole prototype flew on 19 May 1952. Although the wing sweep mechanism worked well, the aircraft experienced other significant problems and the project was subsequently cancelled. *ASM collection*

initial rate of climb at a staggering 13,350ft/min. With the Korean War in progress the navy had high expectations for the Jaguar when the prototype XF10F-1 flew on 19 May 1952. However, they were to be gravely disappointed. The complex wing mechanism actually worked quite well and gave little trouble during flight testing, but everything else was a disaster. There were major problems with the aircraft's handling despite various aerodynamic modifications, but the most serious issue was the J40 engine. When all J40-powered aircraft were grounded in 1953, the XF10F-1 programme was halted and the second prototype was not completed.

One of the other aircraft seriously affected by the failure of the J40 programme was the McDonnell F3H Demon. The advent of high-speed jet bombers presented particular problems for a naval task force. If such a target was detected by radar at a range of 100 miles and above 40,000ft altitude then an interceptor launched from a carrier would need to be able to engage before the bomber reached 20 miles' range. At a bomber speed of 480mph, this only allowed eight minutes for a carrier fighter to start up, launch, climb to above 40,000ft and engage the target. Thus as early as 1948, the navy was looking at the concept of a deck-launched interceptor (DLI) to meet this requirement, and in 1949, two designs were awarded contracts for prototypes, one of which was the F3H Demon. It was to be powered by a single Westinghouse J40 turbojet and was expected to be capable of 644mph at 50,000 feet (Mach 0.97). However, when the prototype XF3H-1 flew on 7 August 1951 it was powered by a non-afterburning J40-WE-6, which produced only 6,500lb thrust instead of the intended J40-WE-8, which would have produced 9,200lb.s.t. The second prototype eventually received the more

Development of the McDonnell F3H Demon began in 1948, when it was seen as a fast climbing day interceptor. The prototype XF3H-1 shown here first flew in August 1951, but the subsequent test programme was marred by several crashes, in which two pilots were killed, and also by the poor performance of the Westinghouse J40 engine. *via Aviation Archives*

A total of fifty-six F3H-1N Demons were produced from late 1953 onwards, but by that time it was realised that the J40 engine was too unreliable for service use and consequently, many never flew but were used as training airframes. This led to the embarrassing situation of completed aircraft being towed through the streets of St Louis for loading onto barges for transport down the Mississippi to Memphis. *William Rudolph collection via Aviation Archives*

powerful engine but both aircraft suffered various problems and were grounded for a time during the test programme. In the meantime, the navy had decided that the Demon should be developed as a general purpose all-weather fighter and this resulted in the F3H-1N, which would be equipped with a Hughes APG-50 radar. This first flew in December 1953, but by then the Westinghouse J40 engine programme was in serious trouble and a proposal to re-engine the Demon with the Allison J71 turbojet rated at 9,700lb.s.t. had been approved. This resulted in the F3H-2N, which first flew on 23 April 1955, and eventually, in 1956, the Demon finally began to equip operational squadrons. A total of 519 Demons were produced, including eighty F2H-2Ms modified to carry Sparrow air-to-air missiles and 239 F2H-2 strike fighters capable of carrying up to 6,000lbs of bombs or rockets.

The other aircraft ordered as a DLI was the delta-winged Douglas F4D Skyray, which was also designed around the Westinghouse J40. However, the prototype XF4D-1, which flew on 23 January 1951, was powered by an Allison J35, giving only 5,000lb thrust. Eventually both prototypes received the intended Westinghouse J40-WEW-8, giving 11,600lb.s.t. with afterburning, and on 3 October 1953, one of these gained the World Air Speed Record with an average speed of 752.944mph – the first time that a naval carrier-capable aircraft had achieved this distinction. Despite this success the troublesome J40 was replaced in production F4D-1 with the Pratt & Whitney J57, which initially offered 9,700lb.s.t., or 14,800lbs, with afterburning. The first of these spectacularly exceeded Mach 1 in level flight during its maiden flight on 5 June 1954, but it was not until mid-1956 that the Skyray finally entered service.

When the navy ordered Demon and Skyray interceptors, a third option was a revised

Despite problems with the J40 engine, two XF3H-1 Demons were deployed for trials aboard the Midway class carrier USS *Coral Sea* (CV43) in October 1953.

By 1954, the Demon programme was in serious trouble and was on the verge of being cancelled. However, McDonnell was permitted to modify two F3H-1N airframes to accept the 9,700lb.s.t. Allison J71-A-2E engine (14,400lb thrust with afterburning), which substantially improved performance to the extent that eventually a total of 461 F3H-2 variants were ordered, although the first of these did not fly until April 1955 and only entered service in late 1956. The ultimate Demon variant was the F3H-2M, which could carry the Sparrow AAM and a four-ship formation of VF(AW)-3 is shown here in 1957.

The Douglas F4D Skyray was a contemporary of the F3H Demon and was also planned around the unfortunate Westinghouse J40 engine. Due to problems with that engine, the first XF4D-1 was powered by a 5,000lb.s.t. Allison J35 engine when it flew on 23 January 1951. Initial carrier trials were carried out aboard the USS Coral Sea (CV43) in October 1953.

When the J40 engine programme was cancelled, Douglas modified the Skyray to accept the Pratt & Whitney J57 engine, which ultimately gave 10,000lb.s.t., boosted to 16,000lb with afterburning. With this engine the Skyray was just capable of exceeding Mach 1 in level flight, although production aircraft retained the F4D-1 designation and were inevitably known as the 'Ford'. The J57-powered Skyray flew in June 1954, but it was not until 1956 that operational squadrons began to receive examples of this fast-climbing interceptor.

An interesting photo taken in 1951 showing a variety of early jet fighters flown by the Naval Air Test Centre at NAS Patuxent River. Leading the formation is the exotic Vought F7U-1 Cutlass, which had flown in prototype form as early as 29 September 1948 and was powered by a pair of Westinghouse J34 turbojets (4,250lb.s.t. with afterburning). Behind it are a McDonnell F2H-1 Banshee, a Grumman F9F-2 Panther and a Vought F6U-1 Pirate.

version of the Vought F7U-1 Cutlass. This was a machine with a chequered history, having been originally ordered in June 1946. It was an unusual twin-engined, tailless swept-wing design based on some German research. Power plant was to be the ubiquitous Westinghouse J34, which powered many early US Navy fighters, and the first XF7U-1 flew on 29 September 1948. Only fourteen production F7U-1s were produced during 1950/51, and these were considered underpowered and difficult to fly, whilst the F7U-2 variant with more powerful engines was cancelled due to development issues with the later versions of the J34 engine. That might have spelt the end of the Cutlass story but the outbreak of the Korean War led to a small order for a developed version, the F7U-3, powered by two 4,600lb.s.t. Westinghouse J46-WE-8A turbojets fitted with afterburners. This engine was basically a scaled-up J34 but was never entirely satisfactory, and the Cutlass was the only airframe in which it was used. The F7U-3 was subsequently developed as a general purpose fighter by the addition of an APQ-36 radar and later with provision for Sparrow air-to-air missiles. The F7U-3 first flew on 20 December 1951 but did not begin to reach operational squadrons until August 1955. Difficult to fly and underpowered, it was not liked by its pilots and by 1957, all had been withdrawn from operational units. More than a quarter of the 307 F7Us built (most of which were the -3 variant) were lost in accidents.

The handling characteristics of the F7U-1 Cutlass left a lot to be desired and consequently, the fourteen production aircraft did not serve at sea. The similar F7U-2 was cancelled and a major redesign, together with more powerful Westinghouse J46 engines, resulted in the F7U-3 (prototype BuAe No.128451 shown here), which flew in December 1951, although this version did not become operational until 1954.

The F7U-3 Cutlass eventually served with four navy squadrons but was used mainly in the attack role. However, it suffered from a very high accident rate and was withdrawn from service as a front-line fighter in 1956/57, although a photo reconnaissance version, the F7U-3P, continued until 1959. This photo shows an F7U-3 of VA-212 aboard USS *Bon Homme Richard* (CVA31), July 1956.

Although many single-seat fighters were adapted for the night fighter role, in 1946 the navy ordered three prototype XF3D-1s as their first carrier based two-seat, all-weather jet fighter. The Douglas design was typical of that era with a mid-mounted straight wing and a pair of Westinghouse J34 turbojets below the wide fuselage, which housed the main fuel tanks and allowed the two crew to sit side by side. Deliveries of the production F3D-1 began in 1950 and these were succeeded in 1951 by the F3D-2, which would be the first version to see action when Marine squadrons VMF(N)-542 and VMF(N)-513 deployed to Korea in 1952. On 2 November 1952, one of these Skyknights became the first jet to destroy another jet in night combat and subsequently VMF(N)-513 was credited with shooting down six Mig-15s without loss to themselves.

The final US Navy fighter of this era was the Grumman F11F-1 Tiger. Originally conceived as the F9F-9, it was redesignated as the F11F-1 when the first of three prototypes flew on 30 July 1954. Its origins lay in a 1952 proposal by Grumman to produce a version of their swept-wing F9F-6 Cougar powered by a 7,600lb.s.t. Wright J65 (Sapphire), but ultimately the result was a completely new aircraft. Initial test results were disappointing as even with the

In 1946, the US Navy ordered a two-seat, all-weather fighter in the form of the Douglas F3D Skyknight and the prototype XF3D-1 flew on 28 March 1948. It was a fairly conventional design with straight wings and twin Westinghouse J34 engines below the wing roots. The wide fuselage allowed the pilot and radar operator to sit side by side and the nose housed a bulky APQ-35 radar.

Main production version of the Skyknight was the F3D-2, which was originally intended to be powered by Westinghouse J46 engines, but development of this powerplant was abandoned and an uprated version of the J34 was used instead. Despite its bulk and limited performance, the Skyknight actually shot down more enemy aircraft in the Korean War (including some Mig-15s) than any other US Navy fighter, although was almost exclusively used by land-based USMC squadrons. The example shown here landing aboard the USS *Shangri-La* (CV38) in 1955 belongs to VX-4, a US Navy test and trials squadron.

The Grumman F11F Tiger evolved from attempts to improve the performance of the F9F-6 Cougar. By the time the prototype flew on 30 July 1954, it was a completely different aircraft, with a thin swept wing and a slim area ruled fuselage. Nevertheless, it was officially designated as the XF9F-9 and was only given its own discrete designation as the XF11F-1 in April 1955, by which time a second prototype and three production aircraft had flown.

The prototype Tiger shown here was powered by a 7,450lb.s.t. Wright J65 W-7 turbojet, a licence-built version of the British Armstrong Siddeley Sapphire axial-flow engine, but production aircraft had the W-18 version, which produced 10,500lb.s.t. with afterburning.

The shape of things to come. The supersonic Chance Vought F8U Crusader resulted from a US Navy requirement for a supersonic air superiority fighter issued in 1952. The first XF8U-1 flew in March 1955, and is shown during subsequent carrier trials.

incorporation of area rule, the Tiger remained subsonic (Mach 0.95), although the later addition of afterburning increased speed to Mach 1.12 at 36,000 feet. In addition, its range turned out to be less than anticipated and with the supersonic Chance Vought F8U Crusader due to fly in 1955, there was little point in persisting with the Tiger. Only 201 were delivered, serving from 1957 but being withdrawn from 1959 onwards. The exception was the navy's Blue Angels aerobatic team, which flew their Tigers from 1957 to 1968.

Chapter Five

A Good Idea at the Time

The early jet engines did not offer significant increases in power over some of the advanced piston engines, although they had advantages at higher altitudes. However, they used considerably more fuel and throttle response was poor as opposed to a piston engine, where opening the throttle produced an immediate response. These considerations, as well as the fact that jets needed a greater take-off and landing distance, were particularly significant for an aircraft intended to operate from aircraft carriers. Consequently, although the US Navy took an early interest in jet development, their thoughts turned to the idea of a mixed-power fighter in which the jet engine provided a boost for take-offs, improved high altitude performance and increased maximum speed when required. At other times, the jet would be shut down to conserve fuel and the aircraft would cruise on its piston engine alone. Two

Due to issues with the early jet engines, the concept of a mixed-power fighter seemed attractive and the result was the Ryan FR-1 Fireball. A General Electric J31 jet engine in the rear fuselage supplemented a conventional Wright R-1850 radial engine in the nose. The Fireball was also the first US Navy fighter to feature a tricycle undercarriage.

distinct types of mixed-power fighters were developed – a relatively compact and lightweight aircraft suitable for operation from the smaller escort carriers and a larger, more powerful fighter intended to operate from the larger fleet carriers. In fact, the navy was hedging its bets because in the same timescale they also sponsored development of pure jet fighters, which resulted in the McDonnell FH-1 Phantom and the North American FJ-1 Fury (see Chapter Three).

The only mixed-power fighter to enter production was the Ryan FR-1 Fireball. Following evaluation of other projects, BuAer placed an order for three XFR-1 Fireballs in early 1943 and the first aircraft flew on 25 June 1944 – a remarkable achievement for a company that previously never built a combat aircraft, let alone one to exacting naval requirements. The Fireball was a simple design with a low-set laminar flow wing and a tricycle undercarriage. Power was provided by a nose-mounted 1,350hp Wright R-1820-72W radial engine and a 1,600lb.s.t. General Electric J31 turbojet in the rear fuselage. The air intakes for the jet were in the wing root leading edges. Maximum speed was only 404mph at 17,800 feet, although service ceiling was 43,100 feet, which represented a substantial increase over the 37,300 feet that the piston-engined Grumman F6F Hellcat could reach, and illustrated the advantage of jet engines in this aspect of performance. By January 1945, no less than 700 Fireballs were on order, but most of these were cancelled after VJ day and only sixty-six production FR-1s were delivered. In March 1945, the first of these went to VF-66, which carried out carrier qualification trials later that year aboard the USS *Ranger* (CV4). Subsequently this unit was

This FR-1 Fireball demonstrates flight on jet power alone, with the piston engine shut down. In practice, the normal procedure was to cruise on the piston engine to extend endurance and to start the jet in combat situations when the extra power was needed.

Fireballs of VF-1E aboard the escort carrier USS *Badoeng Strait* (CVE116) during exercises in the summer of 1947. These provided valuable experience of operating jets at sea but the mixed-power concept offered few advantages and the Fireball was withdrawn from service later that year.

renumbered VF-41 and later VF-1E, and from 1945 to 1947 embarked aboard various escort carriers when taking part in exercises. A development of the Fireball was the XF2R-1, in which the piston engine was replaced by a General Electric XT-31 turboprop delivering 2,300shp and 600lb residual thrust. The prototype flew in November 1946 and demonstrated an increase in speed to around 500mph at sea level, but by that time conventional (and less complex) pure jets offered higher performance.

The other naval mixed-power project was the Curtiss XF-15C, which was larger than the Ryan FR-1 and had more powerful engines in the shape of a 2,100hp Pratt & Whitney R-2800-34W radial engine in the nose and a fuselage-mounted 2,700lb.s.t. Allis-Chalmers J36 turbojet (actually an American-built version of the British de Havilland H1-B Goblin). Three prototypes were ordered in April 1944 and the first XF15C-1 flew on 27 February 1945, but without the jet engine fitted. This aircraft was destroyed in an accident in the following May after the jet engine had been installed. Development issues delayed the delivery of the other two prototypes until November 1947, by which time the US Navy was firmly committed to pure jets and no further orders were forthcoming.

The air force also looked at mixed-power fighters but in this case their requirement was for a long-range fighter to escort the B-29 Superfortress. In this role, although the jet engine

Whereas the Fireball was intended to operate from the smaller carriers, the US Navy also required a similar mixed-power fighter to fly from the larger fleet carriers, and in 1944 it ordered three Curtiss XF15C-1 prototypes.

offered performance enhancements, it would not be able to meet range requirements. The USAAF specification issued in 1943 called for a speed of 500mph, a range of 2,500 miles and a service ceiling of 37,000 feet. Following evaluation of various proposals, two Convair XP-81 prototypes were ordered in February 1944. Convair had been formed in 1943 by the merging of the Consolidated and Vultee companies and their design utilised a fuselage-mounted 4,000lb.s.t. General Electric J33 turbojet and a General Electric XT-31 turboprop in the nose. However, development of the XT-31 was considerably delayed and consequently, when the first XP-81 flew on 7 February 1945, a Packard-built Merlin V-1650-7 piston engine was used instead. Despite the lack of the turboprop the XP-81 demonstrated good handling characteristics, and performance improvements were expected when the Merlin was replaced by the turboprop in December 1945. In fact, the results were disappointing as the XT-31 failed to reach its designed output by a considerable margin. Consequently, orders for thirteen pre-production YP-81s were cancelled and the two XP-81 prototypes were used only for research purposes until 1948, when they were grounded.

Another approach was for the bomber to carry its own escorting fighter, although the idea of a so-called 'parasite fighter' was not new. Between the wars, the US Navy's airships *Akron* and *Macon* were designed to carry four Curtiss F9C-2 Sparrowhawk fighters and towards the end of the Second World War, the idea was revived as a way of providing a jet-powered escort for B-29s and the new B-36 then under development.

One aircraft considered for this requirement was the Northrop XP-79. Founded by John Northrop in the early 1930s, the company had worked to prove the viability of tailless flying

The prototype Convair XP-81 was initially completed in January 1945 with a Packard-built Merlin engine in the nose, and it was not until the following December that the XT31 turboprop was installed, as shown here.

The XP-81 was an exceptionally clean design with a high aspect ratio wing and the jet engine intakes faired into the upper fuselage behind the cockpit. However, the turboprop was a disappointment, producing only 1,650shp instead of the expected 2,300shp, and overall performance was only slightly better than with the Merlin piston engine.

wing aircraft. This led to a contract in 1942 for a rocket-powered interceptor, which later became the XP-79A. Apart from its tailless configuration, the aircraft was unusual in that the pilot was accommodated in a prone position, which it was thought would enable him to tolerate higher G forces. (Britain also investigated this idea in 1954, with a specially modified Meteor.) The most bizarre feature was that the aircraft would destroy enemy bombers by ramming them, the wing leading edges being specially strengthened so that they could cut through wings and tail surfaces of an enemy bomber. Following trials with unpowered gliders, one was fitted with a 2,000lb.s.t. Aerojet rocket motor and made the first rocket-powered flight on 5 July 1944. However, the rocket motor proved unsatisfactory and two XP-79B prototypes, powered by two Westinghouse I-19 (J30) turbojets, were ordered. Also, the idea of ramming tactics had been abandoned and the XP-79B had provision for four 0.5in machine guns. A speed of 547mph and rate of climb of 4,000ft/min was anticipated but these figures were never validated as when the first XP-79B took to the air on 12 September 1945, it crashed only fifteen minutes into the flight, killing its pilot, Harry Crosby. This spelt the end of the project and construction of the second prototype was cancelled.

Slightly more successful was the McDonnell XP-85 Goblin, which was designed to be completely housed within a B-36. To meet this requirement the fighter was designed with

The revolutionary Northrop XP-79 tailless jet fighter offered compact dimensions, partly due to the adoption of a prone pilot layout. The XP-79B was seriously considered in 1944 for the parasite role but the project was abandoned when the prototype crashed on its maiden flight on 12 September 1945, killing the pilot.

Another view of the XP-79B, showing more of its unusual features apart from the tailless configuration and the prone pilot. These included a four-wheeled undercarriage and the intakes at the wing tips, which provided ram air to bellows operating the ailerons.

The air force persisted with the idea of a parasite fighter and in 1945 authorised the McDonnell Aircraft Corporation to proceed with the design of a suitable fighter under the designation XP-85. The requirement for the aircraft to be partially stowed in the forward bomb bay of the Convair B-36 placed tight restrictions on overall dimensions and the result was one of the strangest aircraft ever flown. The almost completed prototype is shown here in the summer of 1948.

The XP-85 was designed to be carried on a trapeze, which would lower the aircraft for release and hoist it back in after recovery. This system was tested in a factory mock-up during 1947/48.

The first free flight of the XP-85 took place on 23 August 1948. The aircraft was released from the modified B-29, which acted as the mothership, but the pilot, Edwin Schoch, was unable to hook on again to the trapeze and was forced to land on the Muroc lake bed. Subsequently the two prototypes made a total of only seven free flights, of which only three resulted in successful hook-ons. A review resulted in the project being cancelled on 25 October 1949.

folding swept wings and triple vertical tail surfaces (very advanced thinking for the time), and after further work a contract for two prototype XF-85 Goblins was issued in March 1947. The first prototype was damaged during wind tunnel tests and so it was the second prototype that made the first free flight on 28 August 1948. The XF-85 was powered by single Westinghouse J34 axial-flow turbojet and a maximum speed of 648mph was optimistically forecast, although no high-speed testing was ever completed.

However, the idea of a parasite fighter was not completely abandoned and in 1953, a Republic RF-84F Thunderflash was modified so that it could be carried by a RB-36F. Although it weighed over four times as much as the diminutive XF-85, the then current versions of the B-36 were powered by four pod-mounted General Electric J47 turbojets in addition to the original six Pratt & Whitney R-4360-41 turbo compound radial engines and so were well able to lift the greater weight. The parasite-carrying bomber version was designated GRB-36F FICON (Fighter Conveyer) and modifications to the GRF-84F fighter were minimal, consisting of the addition of a retractable nose hook to engage the bomber's trapeze and an anhedral

In 1953, the latest B-36F version of the intercontinental bomber was modified to carry a single Republic RF-84F Thunderflash photo reconnaissance fighter. The combination was briefly used operationally in 1955/56.

tailplane to clear the lower edges of the bomb bay. Although improving on the XF-85 experience, the operation of the Thunderstreak from the GRB-36F bomber was still difficult, although twenty-five GRF-84Fs (later designated RF-84K) were produced and served with the 91st Strategic Reconnaissance Squadron from 1955 to 1956.

When swept wings were introduced after the war it was realised that they suffered from serious handling issues at low speeds. At high angles of attack the wing tips would stall before the rest of the wing, and this caused the centre of lift to shift dramatically forward, which in turn caused the angle of attack to increase even more with the result that the aircraft would become uncontrollable and crash. Subsequently various aerodynamic developments such as slats and wing fences helped to overcome this problem but in designing the XF-91 Thunderceptor, Republic's solution was more drastic. Instead of wing thickness and chord tapering outwards from the wing root, this conventional arrangement was reversed so that the wing tips were thicker and broader than the inner sections. This arrangement prevented the tip from stalling before the rest of the wing and made the handling more predictable. First flown in May 1949, the XF-91 was a high-speed jet interceptor loosely based on the F-84F airframe but boosted by a Reaction Motors XLR-11 four-motor rocket system clustered around the tail. Coupled with the 5,200lb.s.t. General Electric J47 turbojet, this endowed the XF-91 with a spectacular, albeit short duration, performance and in December 1952, it became the first US

In May 1949, Republic flew the prototype XF-91 Thunderceptor, which superficially resembled the Thunderstreak but its swept wings incorporated a reverse taper feature where the outboard sections were thicker and had a wider chord than the inner sections.

As its name implied, XF-91 was designed primarily as an interceptor and was powered by a single 5,200lb.s.t. General Electric J47-GE-3 turbojet, but an additional 6,000lb thrust was available for short periods from four XLR-11-RM-9 rocket motors, the arrangement of which is shown in this photo. Also visible here are the unusual twin-wheel bogies of the main undercarriage.

127

The prototype XF-91 (46680) banks away to show the unusual wing configuration. With afterburning and the rocket motors running, the XF-91 could reach almost 1,000mph but its endurance was only a maximum of twenty-five minutes, so despite its impressive performance, no production orders were forthcoming.

Although no orders were forthcoming, the two XF-91 prototypes continued flying for test and research purposes until 1954, and both underwent various modifications. The first prototype (at left) was fitted with a radome and a chin air intake, whilst the second (at right) was seriously damaged by fire in 1951 as a result of a take-off incident and was rebuilt with a Vee tail. *via Aviation Archives*

combat aircraft to exceed Mach 1 in level flight. Despite this, no production order was placed as the USAF was prepared to wait for other more capable aircraft then being developed.

By late 1944, British planning staffs were beginning to look ahead to a greater involvement in the Pacific theatre. Given the nature of the area, there were obvious attractions to the concept of a seaplane fighter. Saunders Roe produced a proposal as early as 1943 for a single-seat, twin-engined jet flying boat fighter. Subsequently the MAP issued specification E.6/44 based on this work and the result was the SR.A/1, the first of three prototypes flying on 16 July 1947. The A/1 was unique in that it was the only application for the Metropolitan Vickers MVB.1 Beryl axial-flow turbojet, which offered 3,250lb.s.t., increasing to 3,850lb in the MVB.2, which powered the third prototype. Despite its rather portly outline due to the flying boat hull, the SR.A/1 achieved a respectable maximum speed to 516mph and a rate of climb in excess of 4,000ft/min. However, by the time the prototypes were flying, the Pacific War was long since over and neither the RAF or RN had any requirement for a seaplane fighter. Testing continued, but in August 1949, the third prototype was lost when it struck a piece of flotsam when alighting on the waters of the Solent. Later that year, the second prototype was lost in an accident off Felixstowe, the cause being attributed to pilot disorientation while carry out aerobatics. These accidents effectively terminated the programme.

On the other hand, the US Navy continued to maintain an interest in waterborne aircraft. Mostly these were large flying boats for maritime patrol and anti-submarine warfare, but in 1948, BuAer issued specification OS-114 for an experimental seaplane fighter. As originally envisaged, this would have been a two-seat night/all-weather fighter and the successful bidder was Convair, who investigated the characteristics of both blended hull and retractable hydro

As early as 1943, Saunders Roe had proposed a jet-powered flying boat fighter. An order for three prototypes was placed in May 1944 under the designation SR.A/1, the first of these eventually flying on 16 July 1947.

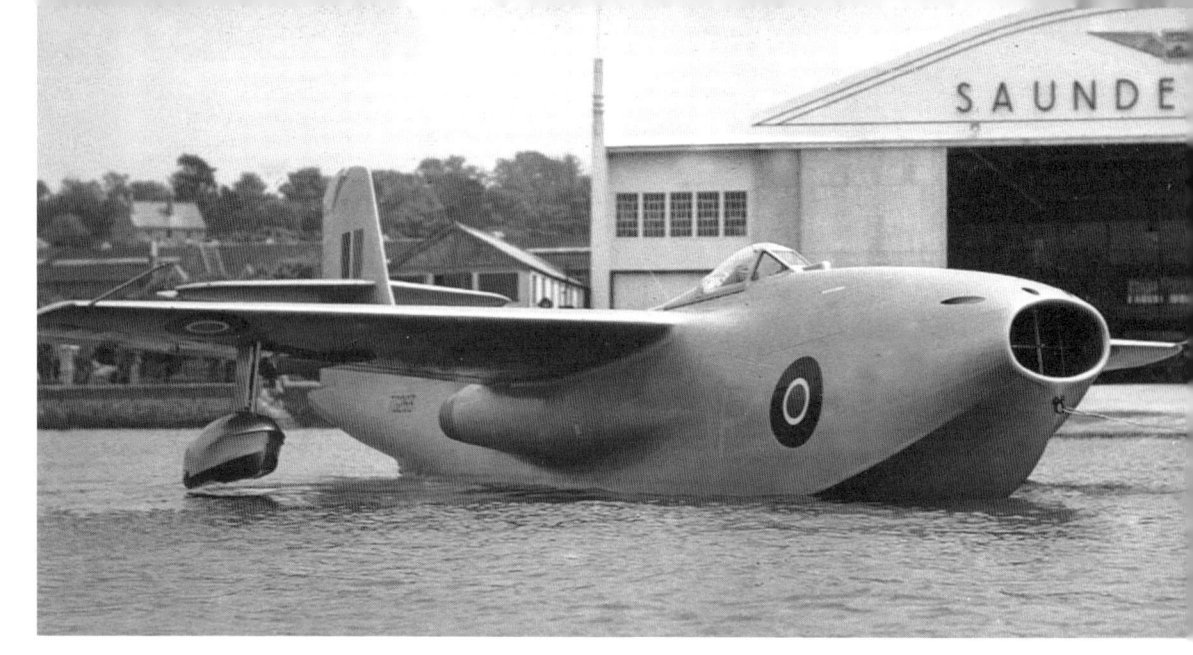

The first Saunders Roe SR.A/1 (TG263) afloat at Cowes in the summer of 1947. Points of interest included the elevated air intake to avoid spray ingestion on take-off, jet exhaust pipes on either side of the fuselage, retractable wing floats and provision for four nose-mounted 20mm cannon above the intake. *ASM collection*

In the immediate post-war era, the US Navy envisaged waterborne fighters as being useful to protect amphibious operations and thereby reduce the need for supporting aircraft carriers. Eventually, orders were placed for a Convair delta-winged fighter, which utilised retractable hydro skis for take-off and landing. Two prototypes designated XF2Y-1 were ordered in January 1951.

The Convair XF2Y-1 Seadart was designed to be powered by two Westinghouse J46 engines, but problems with this powerplant led to the lower rated J34s being installed for the early test flights.

The delta-winged Seadart drew on Convair's experience with the land-based F-92 and F-102 programmes, but was twin-engined, the intakes being positioned on top of the fuselage to avoid spray ingestion. However, even with J46 engines installed, it was not supersonic due to lack of area ruling.

A third aircraft designated as YF2Y-1 was flown in March 1955, and various twin and single ski configurations were tested in a programme involving over 300 flights, which came to an end in 1956. A further two YF2Y-1s had been completed but not flown, and the four remaining airframes have all been preserved and are currently on display at various museums. Here one of the Seadarts earmarked for preservation is embarked on the carrier USS *Essex* (CV09) together with a batch of surplus F9F Panthers while on passage to an East Coast port in 1957.

ski configurations, with the latter eventually adopted. Further interest in a seaplane fighter would have lapsed except for the outbreak of the Korean War. Convair then produced a revised design for a single-seat, delta-winged fighter based on their F-102, and a contract for two prototypes was awarded in January 1951. The prototype XF2Y-1 Seadart officially made its first flight (having previously become briefly airborne during high-speed taxi trials) on 9 April 1953 and was powered by two Westinghouse J34-E-32 engines rated at 3,400lb.s.t., although production aircraft were intended to have the 6,100lb.s.t. Westinghouse J46. The second Seadart was completed as a YF2Y-1 with these engines and in August 1954, exceeded Mach 1 in a shallow dive, making it the world's only supersonic seaplane! However, this aircraft was lost when it went out of control during an air display at San Diego. The original XF2Y-1, now re-engined with the J46, continued to fly for research purposes until 1958, but neither the navy nor the air force had a requirement for such an aircraft and the project was abandoned.

Photo Credits

Unless otherwise credited, all the images in this book are from the US National Archive and Research Agency (NARA) and are held in their Still Image facility at College Park, Maryland. Photos from the author's own archives are credited to Air Sea Media (ASM).

Several individuals have assisted with the provision of other images, including Tim Kershaw of the Jet Age Museum at Gloucester/Staverton airport, Ron Downey of the US-based Aviation Archive, and the well-known aviation photographer Peter March. These and other sources are credited as appropriate.

Bibliography

Birtles, Philip, *de Havilland Vampire, Venom and Sea Vixen*, Ian Allan, 1986.

Birtles, Philip, *Supermarine Attacker, Swift and Scimitar*, Ian Allan, 1982.

Friedman, Norman, *Fighters over the Fleet*, Seaforth Publishing, 2016.

Golly, John, *Genisis of the Jet*, Airlife, 1996.

Green, William & Cross, Roy, *The Jet Aircraft of the World*, Macdonald & Co, 1956.

Gunston, Bill, *World Encyclopedia of Aero Engines*, Patrick Stephens Ltd, 1985.

Robertson, Bruce (Ed), *United States Army and Air Force Fighters 1916–1961*, Harleyford Publications Ltd, 1961.

Shacklady, Edward, *The Gloster Meteor*, MacDonald & Co, 1962.

Swanborough, Gordon & Bowers, Peter, *United States Military Aircraft since 1909*, revised edition, 1989.

Swanborough, Gordon & Bowers, Peter, *United States Navy Aircraft since 1911*, Putnam, revised edition, 1976.

Thetford, Owen, *Aircraft of the Royal Air Force since 1918*, Putnam, 9th ed, 1995.

Thetford, Owen, *British Naval Aircraft since 1912*, Putnam, revised edition, 1978.

Wagner, Ray, *The North American Sabre*, MacDonald & Co, 1963.